Watercolor

for the first time®

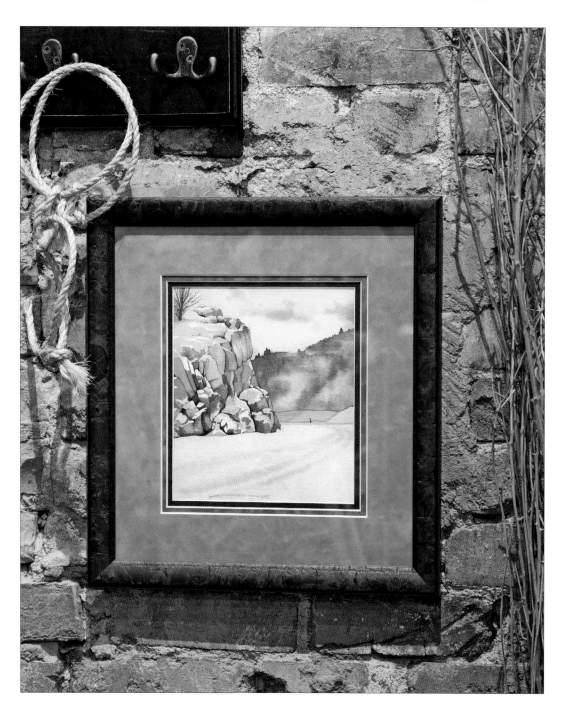

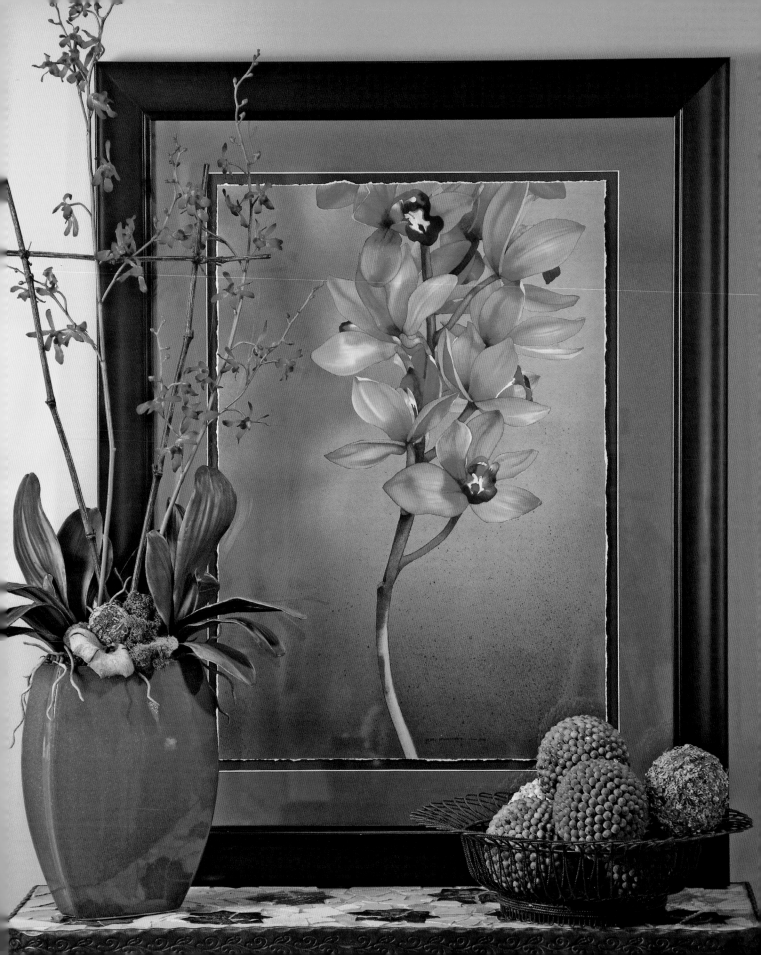

Watercolor

Kory Fluckiger   for the first time®

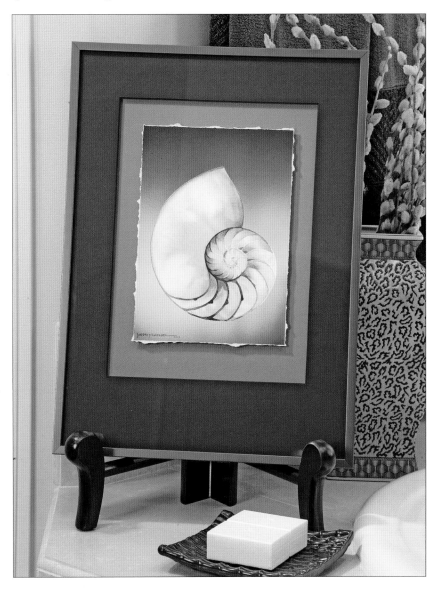

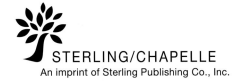

STERLING/CHAPELLE

An imprint of Sterling Publishing Co., Inc.

New York / London
www.sterlingpublishing.com

Chapelle, Ltd., Inc., P.O. Box 9252, Ogden, UT 84409
(801) 621-2777 • (801) 621-2788 Fax
e-mail: chapelle@chapelleltd.com
Web site: www.chapelleltd.com

Every effort has been made to ensure that all information in this book is accurate. However, due to differing conditions, tools, and individual skills, the publisher cannot be responsible for any injuries, losses, and/or other damages which may result from the use of the information in this book.

Due to limited amount of available space, we must print our patterns at a reduced size in order to give our patrons the maximum number of patterns possible in our publications. We believe the quality and quantity of our patterns will compensate for any inconvenience this may cause.

This volume is meant to stimulate craft ideas. If readers are unfamiliar or not proficient in a skill necessary to attempt a project, we urge that they refer to an instructional book specifically addressing the required technique.

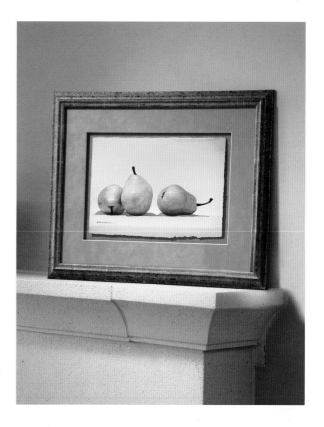

Library of Congress Cataloging-in-Publication Data

Fluckiger, Kory.
 Watercolor for the first time / Kory Fluckiger.
    p. cm.
"A Sterling/Chapelle Book."
 Includes index.
 ISBN 1-4027-2214-1
1. Watercolor painting--Technique. I. Title.

ND2420.F62 2005
751.42'2--dc22
                                                    2005012841

10 9 8 7 6 5 4 3 2 1

Published by Sterling Publishing Co., Inc.
387 Park Avenue South, New York, NY 10016
©2005 by Kory Fluckiger
Distributed in Canada by Sterling Publishing
c/o Canadian Manda Group, 165 Dufferin Street
Toronto, Ontario, Canada M6K 3H6
Distributed in the United Kingdom by GMC Distribution Services
Castle Place, 166 High Street, Lewes, East Sussex, England BN7 1XU
Distributed in Australia by Capricorn Link (Australia) Pty. Ltd.
P.O. Box 704, Windsor, NSW 2756, Australia

Printed in China
All Rights Reserved

Sterling ISBN-13: 978-1-4027-2214-1 (hardcover)
        ISBN-10: 1-4027-2214-1

Sterling ISBN-13: 978-1-4027-5393-0 (paperback)
        ISBN-10: 14027-5393-4

For information about custom editions, special sales, premium
and corporate purchases, please contact Sterling Special Sales Department at
800-805-5489 or specialsales@sterlingpublishing.com.

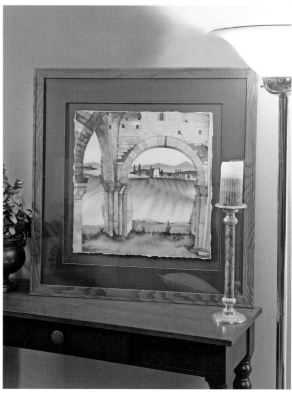

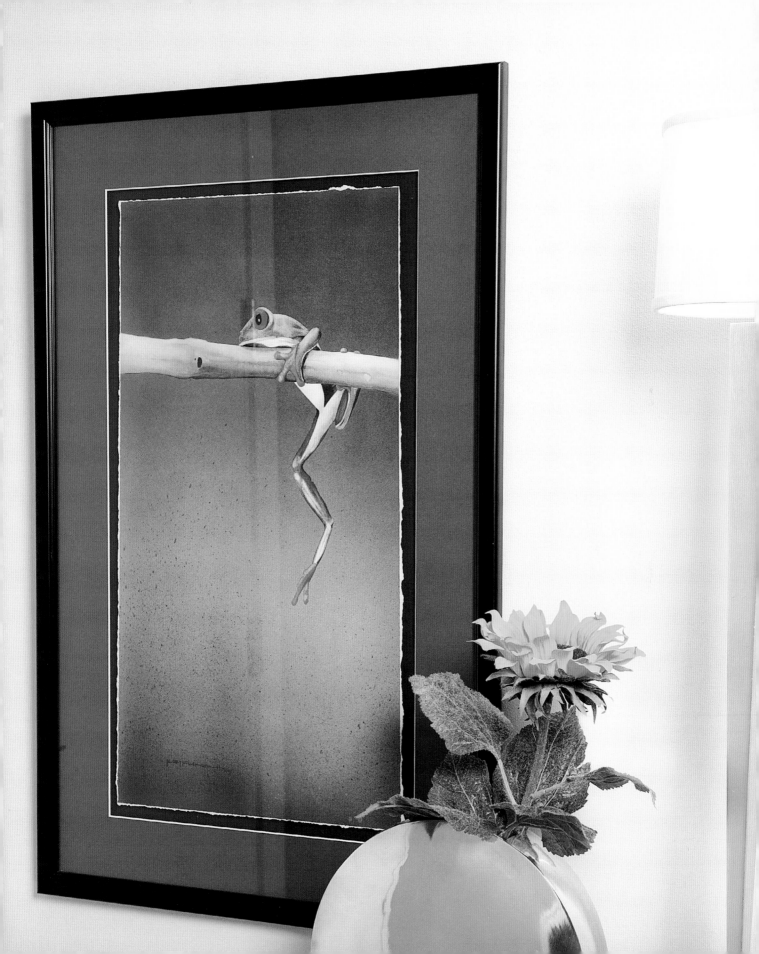

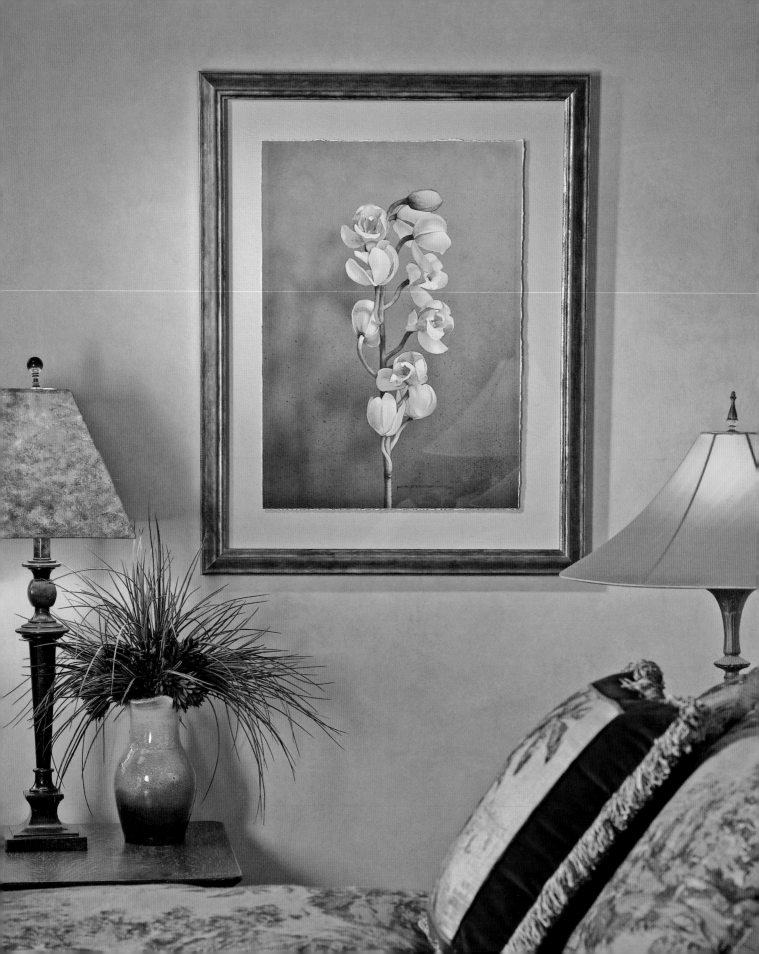

Table of Contents

Introduction

Watercolor painting has been practiced since the development of paper by the Chinese circa 100 A.D. Considered for centuries to be a drawing or sketching medium, watercolor paints have gone through several changes to arrive at the product used today.

One of the first paper centers in the world was located in Fabriano, Italy, where watercolor paints quickly developed. Buon fresco, or wall painting on wet plaster, with watercolor paints soon arose as a form of watercolor painting. One of the most celebrated painters in history, Michelangelo Buonarroti, was a watercolorist. The famous ceiling of the Sistine Chapel painted by Michelangelo between 1508 and 1514 is, in fact, a watercolor.

A truly diverse medium, watercolor painting ranges from abstract and nonrepresentational to nearly photorealism. Many watercolor styles have the familiar look of colors melting into one another, with telltale outlines between shapes, while other styles are characterized by sharper edges.

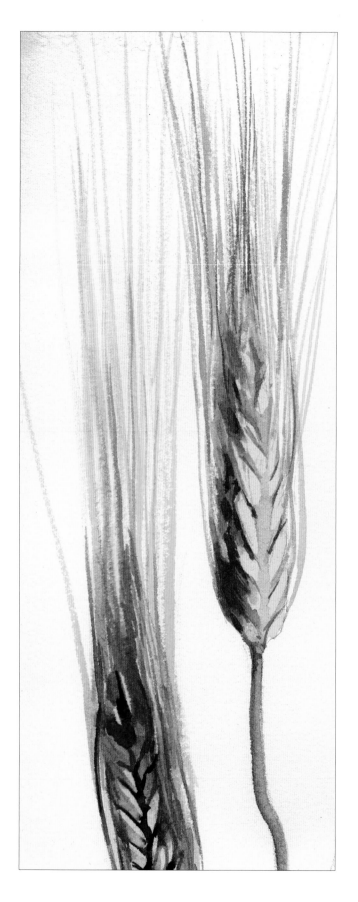

How To Use This Book

Watercolor for the first time® will give you all the basic information necessary to get started in the art of watercolor painting. The projects in this book employ simple, controlled techniques and focus on realism without becoming too wrapped up in minor detail.

Section 1: Getting Started, will familiarize you with the supplies and preparations necessary for beginning your journey as a watercolor artist. Section 2: Basic Techniques, will teach you the fundamentals, or the building blocks, upon which each subsequent project will rest. Section 3: Beyond the Basics, expands on and combines basic techniques to create more complex projects. Section 4: Gallery, will display some of the beautiful pieces that can result from practice and perseverance as a watercolorist.

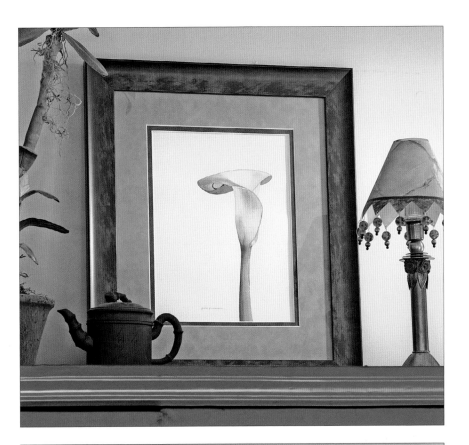

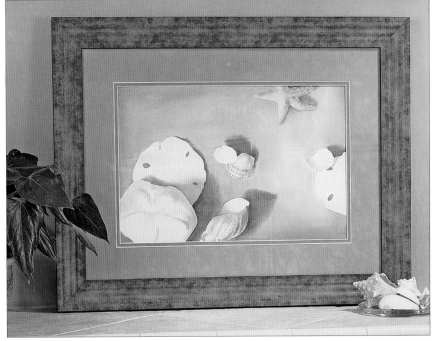

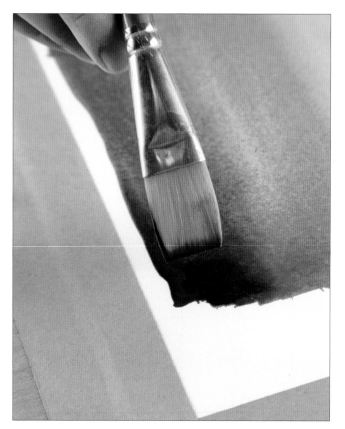

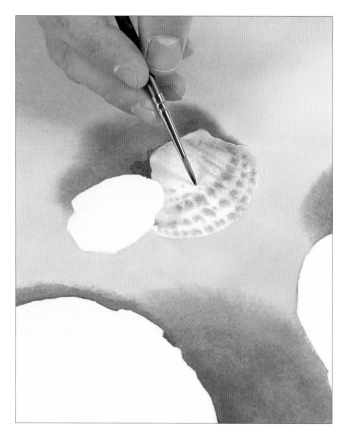

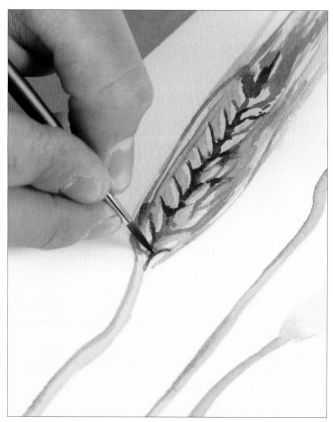

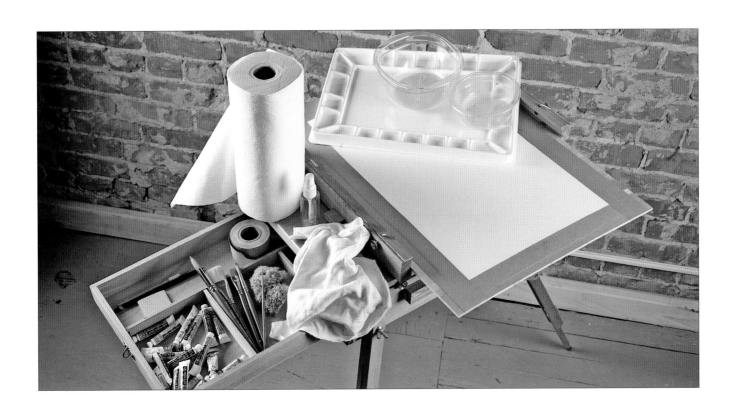

Section 1: *Getting Started*

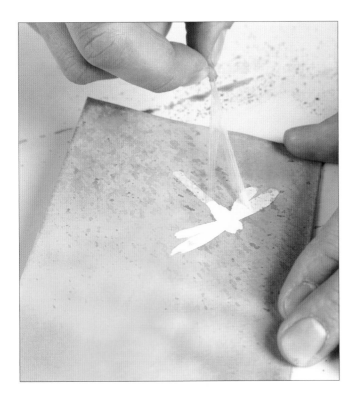

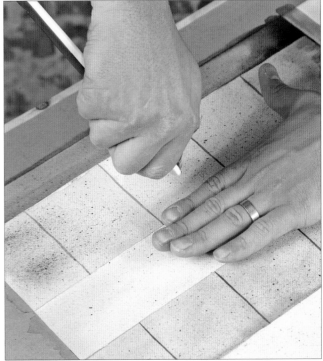

Basic Materials

Art tape: Low-tack, acid-free art tape is used for taping off smaller areas of the watercolor paper. Although similar to masking tape, art tape is less likely to damage your paper upon removal. Always test art tape on a small scrap of watercolor paper before using, to ensure the paper does not tear.

Brushes: It is recommended that you have a variety of brush sizes and shapes. Here are some suggestions:

$\frac{1}{2}$"–1" flats are used for covering large areas of the paper.

#1 round is used for fine detailed painting.

#4, #10, and #14 rounds are used for varying degrees of detailed painting.

Craft knife or razor blade: A good craft knife or razor blade is used to remove the gummed paper tape that holds the watercolor paper to the plywood board.

Disposable brush: The liquid masking fluid has a tendency to clog and destroy brushes. Use a brush that can be thrown away if ruined.

Gum eraser: This nonabrasive eraser will remove graphite without tearing the watercolor paper. Abrasive erasers can damage the paper, as well as cause it to take paint differently.

Gummed paper tape: This tape is used to hold watercolor paper to a plywood board during the stretching process.

Liquid masking fluid: Liquid masking fluid is used to cover spaces that will remain white or be filled in later.

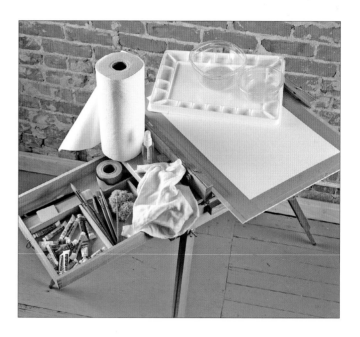

Paper towels: Paper towels are used to soak up excess paint or water. The more-cloth-like paper towels will not fall apart as easily or leave lint on your work.

Pencil: It is important to use a soft-lead pencil, such as a 2B or 4B. Pencils with an H are harder, more difficult to erase, and will tear the watercolor paper more easily. A #2 pencil is known as an HB, which is in the middle of the pencil lead range.

Plastic watercolor palette: A palette with individual compartments around the perimeter and a large, flat mixing area in the center is suggested. A lid is optional, as the paints can dry in the palette and still remain usable after several years. *Note: It is very important that you are comfortable with your palette. Painting will be easier if the palette is of a manageable size and the colors can be easily arranged for convenient mixing.*

Plywood board: An 18" x 24" x $\frac{1}{8}$"–$\frac{1}{4}$" piece of plywood is used to stretch the watercolor paper. Paper stretching is a very important process in this medium, as it renders the paper taut enough for smooth watercolor painting. If you are using watercolor paper of a different size, use a plywood board that is 1"–2" larger than the paper. These boards can be reused once a painting has been removed.

Sea sponge: A natural sea sponge is used to wet large areas of the watercolor paper for stretching.

Spray/mist bottle: A small spray bottle is used to keep your palette wet, or to mist the watercolor paper.

Straightedge ruler: A straightedge is used to evenly tear watercolor paper to the desired size. A metal straightedge is preferred, as it will create a clean edge without tearing the paper.

Toothbrush: A toothbrush with the bristles trimmed to half their original length is used for spattering.

Transparent tape: Transparent tape can be used during the image transferring process to tape the photocopied image to the watercolor paper.

Water basin: Any disposable dish will suffice. Keep in mind that larger basins will more greatly diffuse pigments, and the water will not need to be changed as often. It is a good idea to have two basins for water sources: one for rinsing brushes and one for clean, clear water.

Watercolor paints in tubes: Watercolor paints are made specifically for this type of painting, on watercolor paper. Although each tube can cost anywhere from $4–$20 (US), the paint can last for several years when properly maintained.

Watercolor paper: Watercolor paper is available in many different weights. The most common and most easily acquired is a 140 lb. weight. Most of the painting in this book was produced on 140 lb. cold-pressed paper. Cold-pressed paper generally has a slightly rougher texture, which is what I prefer, as it more readily accepts water. The standard size sheet is 22" x 30", but many other sizes are available. The projects in this book will use 15" x 22" half-sheets.

Workspace: A clean flat workspace, which allows for free movement around the painting, is ideal. I use a collapsible French easel; however, a tabletop will suffice.

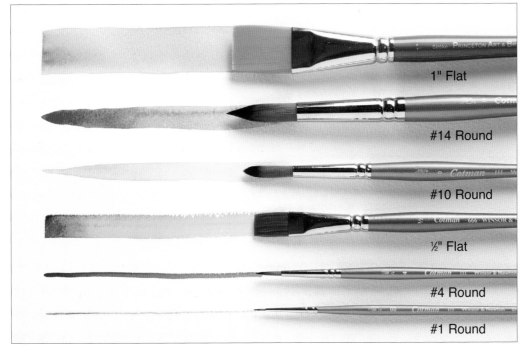

1" Flat

#14 Round

#10 Round

½" Flat

#4 Round

#1 Round

Palette Preparation

It is important that colors on the palette be deliberately laid out and arranged for comfortable mixing. The layout I use has proven very efficient for me, and is based on color theory. If you decide to experiment with your palette, you should know a few things about color theory first.

A band of colors in the visible spectrum can be arranged to show progression in a *color wheel*. Color wheels can range from very simple, including primary and secondary colors, to very complex, including analogous and tertiary, or intermediate, colors. The primary colors are red, yellow, and blue, and cannot be created by mixing any other color combinations. Orange, green, and purple are secondary colors, and are the result of combining two primary colors. Tertiary colors are the product of mixing a primary color with a secondary color, and result in such colors as red-orange, or blue-green.

Colors opposite each other on the color wheel are called complementary colors, while colors next to each other are called analogous colors. Complementary colors placed side by side create a striking contrast, and tend to make each other appear very bright. Analogous colors create visual harmony. A monochromatic color scheme is based on different shades of the same color. The arrangement of paint used here is based on analogous color schemes, as it makes it more convenient to mix similar colors and change hues or saturation quickly. *Note: A **hue** is the pure color. Tints and shades are values of a color. For example: red is a hue and pink is a tint of red. **Saturation** is determined by the purity of a color. The more diluted a particular hue becomes by adding another color, the less saturated it is.*

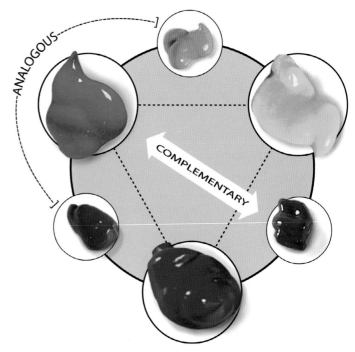

Materials:

- Plastic watercolor palette
- Watercolor paints
  - Alizarin Crimson
  - Burnt Sienna
  - Burnt Umber
  - Cadmium Orange
  - Cadmium Red
  - Cadmium Yellow Light
  - Cerulean Blue
  - Cobalt Blue
  - Dioxazine Violet
  - Green Gold
  - Hooker's Green Deep
  - Ivory Black
  - Raw Sienna
  - Raw Umber
  - Ultramarine Blue
  - Van Dyke Brown
  - Viridian
  - Yellow Ochre

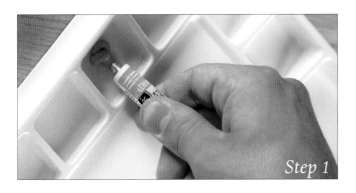

Step 1

1. Squeeze a small drop of paint into the palette sections. *Note: It is not necessary to fill the palette sections.*

2. Allow palette to dry for approximately one hour before beginning to paint. *Note: Otherwise, the brush will become loaded with too much paint.*

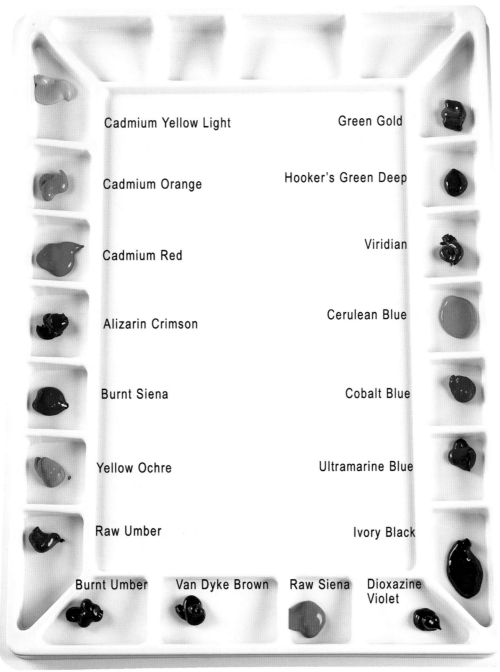

Cadmium Yellow Light

Cadmium Orange

Cadmium Red

Alizarin Crimson

Burnt Siena

Yellow Ochre

Raw Umber

Green Gold

Hooker's Green Deep

Viridian

Cerulean Blue

Cobalt Blue

Ultramarine Blue

Ivory Black

Burnt Umber   Van Dyke Brown   Raw Siena   Dioxazine Violet

Paper Stretching

Most watercolor papers come bearing a watermark of the manufacturer's logo. Hold the paper up to a bright light or window. The watermark usually appears in the lower right-hand corner. Turn the paper so the watermark reads forward. This is the painting surface. Lightly mark the back of the paper with a pencil if you intend to tear or cut the paper before stretching, in order to remember which side to paint on.

Materials:

- Clear water
- Gummed paper tape
- Pencil
- Plywood board
- Ruler or other straightedge
- Sea sponge
- Watercolor paper

Tearing

For most of the projects in this book, you will need to reduce the paper size in the following manner:

1. On a flat surface, fold a sheet of paper in half.

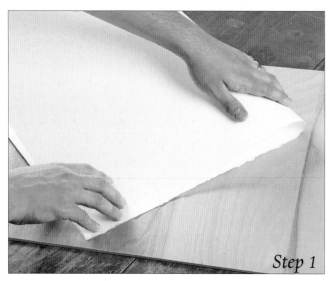

Step 1

2. Carefully crease only the edges that mark the halfway point.

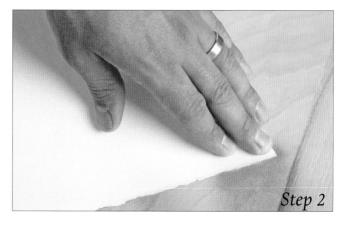

Step 2

3. Unfold the paper and lay the straightedge along the crease.

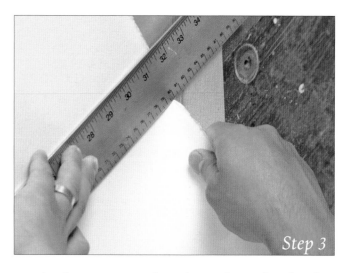

Step 3

4. Apply pressure to the ruler with one hand and gently lift paper with other hand, tearing along the straightedge.

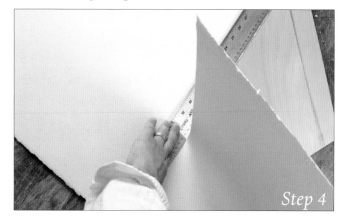

Step 4

Stretching

1. Lay a half-sheet of paper on the plywood board, leaving a margin on all sides.

2. Using the sponge, thoroughly saturate the paper with water, making certain the entire surface is sodden.

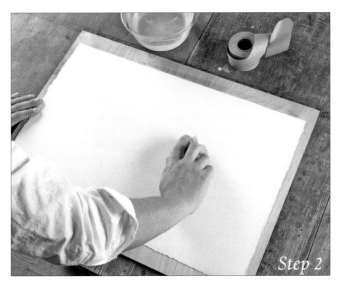

3. Turn the paper over and repeat. *Note: Make certain there are no dry patches, as they may warp the paper as it dries.*

4. Leave the paper on the board for 10–15 minutes, adjusting the wrinkles that appear as the paper stretches.

5. To adjust these "waves," lift one side of the paper at a time and roll it smoothly back onto the board. Repeat this process a few times as necessary.

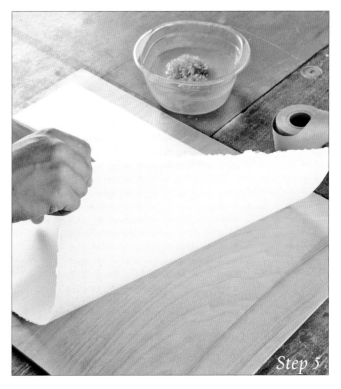

6. While paper is stretching and between "wave" adjustments, measure one length of gummed tape for each side of the paper and tear it off.

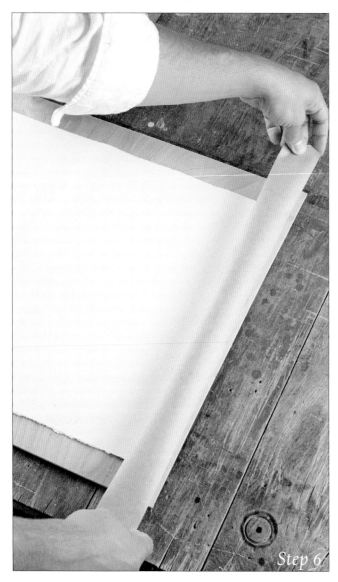

Step 6

7. Set tape aside until paper is fully stretched. *Note: Make certain to not wet the tape, as this will activate the glue.* The paper is ready to mount when it is almost dry to the touch. If in doubt, wait the full 15 minutes previously mentioned.

8. Make certain the paper is as centered on the board as possible, with the correct side facing up.

9. Hold one strip of tape at the edge of the work surface, with the shiny glue side up.

10. Wet the sponge and press onto glue surface.

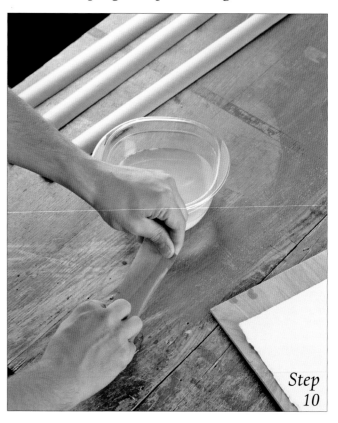

Step 10

11. Slide the tape under the wet sponge to moisten the entire length of tape.

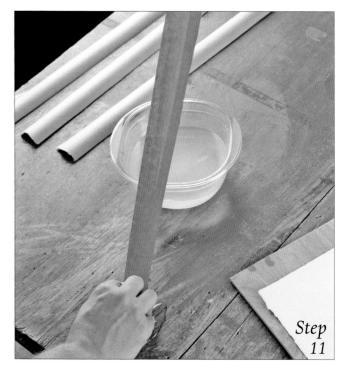

Step 11

12. Position the tape so that half of it is over the paper and half is over the board.

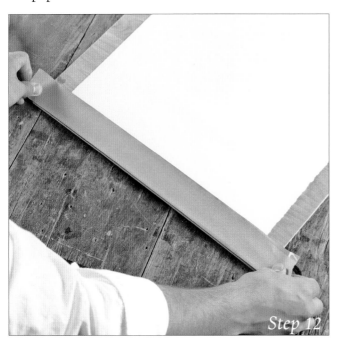

Step 12

13. Place the tape on the paper and board. Press the tape smoothly from the center outward.

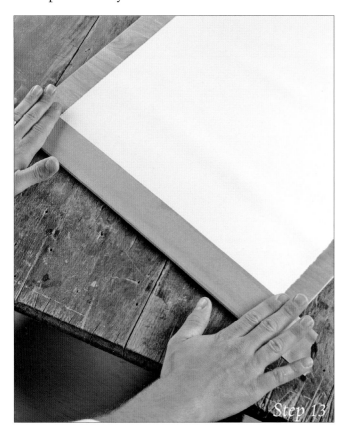

Step 13

14. Repeat for the remaining three sides.

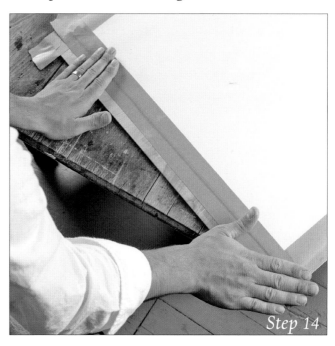

Step 14

15. Allow paper to dry for several hours or overnight. *Note: As the paper dries, it will shrink back to its original size.*

The tape will hold the edges, so as the paper shrinks, the board will flex. *Note: The paper will sometimes raise up to 2" off the board's center. This will reduce bumpiness and help prevent pools of paint from forming, so the painting surface will be smooth and even.*

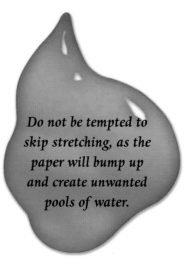

Do not be tempted to skip stretching, as the paper will bump up and create unwanted pools of water.

Image Transferring

Reproductions of the projects have been provided for tracing and transferring onto watercolor paper. Full-color reproductions for techniques can be found in the Section 2 opener on pages 22–23, while the first provided image for each of the projects in Section 3 is what should be copied. Simply follow these instructions, step by step, for each painting.

Materials:

- Art tape or transparent tape
- Pencil
- Photocopied image
- Stretched watercolor paper
- Tracing paper

1. Using a pencil and tracing paper, trace the image from the page in the book.

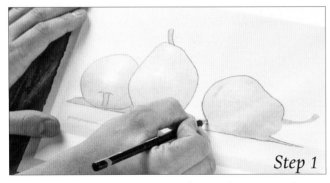

Step 1

2. Photocopy the traced image. Enlarge or reduce as desired.

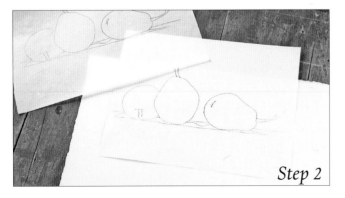

Step 2

3. Using a soft-lead pencil in the HB to 6B range, cover the back of the photocopied image with graphite. *Note: Essentially, this creates custom carbon paper.*

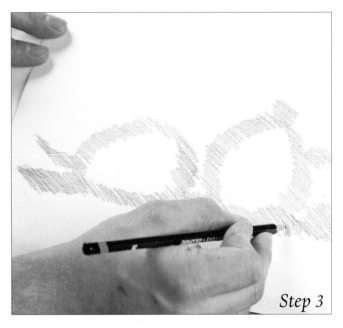

Step 3

4. Using art tape, secure the photocopy, with the graphite face down, to watercolor paper.

5. Firmly trace along image lines.

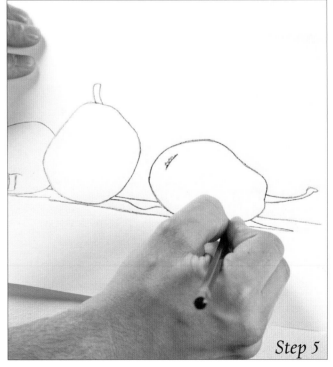

Step 5

6. Remove the tape and photocopied image.

7. Lightly trace over the lines on the watercolor paper to make them a bit more defined.

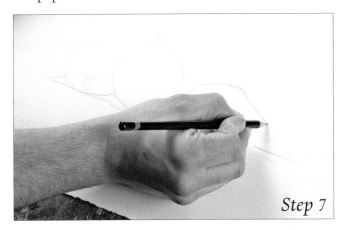

Step 7

8. Press the gum eraser over the drawing, then pull it back up again to "lift" a bit of pencil off the paper. *Note: This will lighten the drawing, so there are few or no lines left once the painting is finished. Avoid lightening so much that the lines cannot be seen, however, as this will result in unwanted guesswork.*

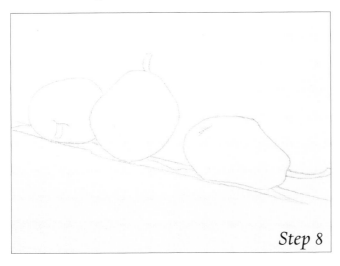

Step 8

Note: It is necessary to trace over the lines on the watercolor paper, and then lighten them again with the eraser for two reasons. If you do not trace over lines once transferred, the graphite can easily brush off the page if you are not careful. It is important to lighten the lines with an eraser afterward, so that too much graphite does not remain trapped under the paint once you begin working.

Caring for Your Brushes

Rinsing watercolor paintbrushes is an important part of maintaining their lifespan. Rinse brushes whenever switching to a new color, or after you are finished using it. Always lay the brush flat, and do not let it stand in water. This may bend the bristles and cause permanent damage.

A Few Things to Consider

The watercolor paints used in this book are a transparent medium. As there is no white paint, the paper must act as the white. Plan for white spots, because once they are gone, there is no recovering them.

Due to their transparent qualities, light reflected off the paper gives watercolor a certain luminescence. This can be used as an advantage, once you learn when to quit. Without proper planning, that luminescent quality can be lost and the painting will become muddy.

It is also important to remember that watercolors dry much lighter than when first applied. It is helpful to experiment with various papers to see how much change will take place in color hues and values. A piece of scrap paper from the same type of paper being used for your painting will prove quite useful.

Finally, many people who have tried watercolor might say it is a medium requiring a great deal of patience. Patience will be required if you want to learn to paint in order to sell your work and make a living. However, if you are willing to relax and delight simply in the act of creating art, then you are ready to more thoroughly enjoy this book and the watercolor painting process.

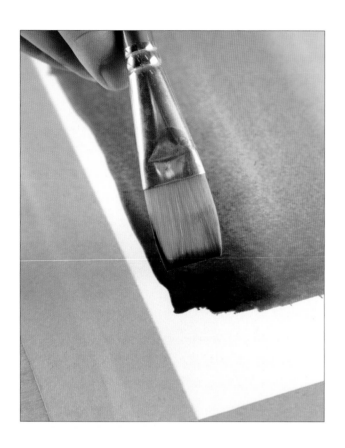

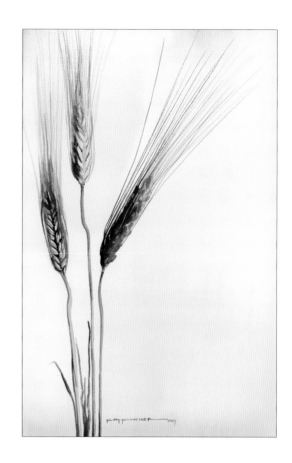

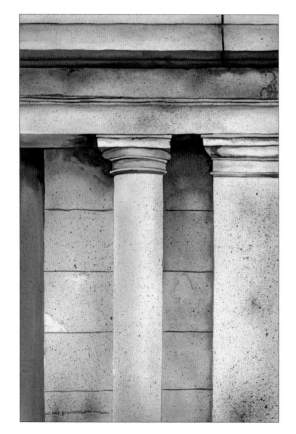

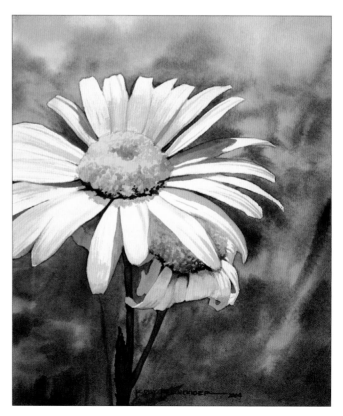

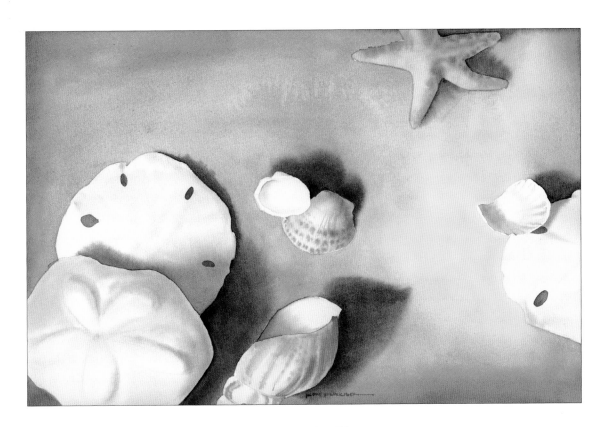

Section 2: *The Basics*

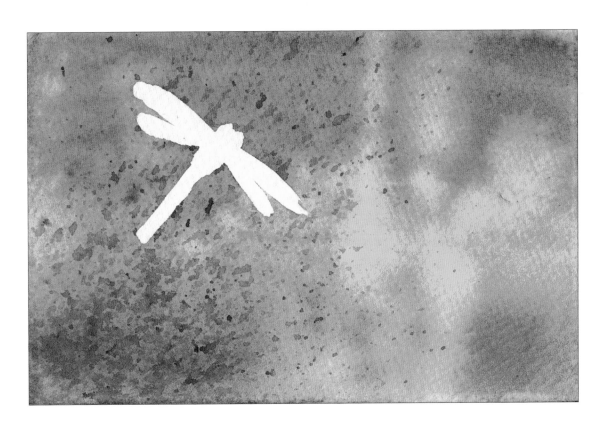

1
Technique

How do I paint using a basic wash?

The basic wash is easily the most important watercolor technique, yet it is also one of the most enjoyable. In this exercise, the finished product will not be a picture, so just relax and have fun. Try to get a feel for how the paint works, which brushes you like best, which colors mix better, and so on.

Materials:

- Brushes: #1 round, #4 round, #10 round, #14 round, $\frac{1}{2}$" flat, 1" flat

- Clear water basin

- Craft knife or razor blade

- Eraser

- Paper towel

- Pencil

- Prepared watercolor palette (Refer to Palette Preparation on pages 14–15)

- Rinse water basin

- Sea sponge

- Spray bottle

- Watercolor paper, 15" x 22"

1. Tear and stretch your watercolor paper. Refer to Paper Stretching instructions on pages 16–17.

2. Mist the palette with the spray bottle. *Note: This will begin to soften the paints and ready them for use.*

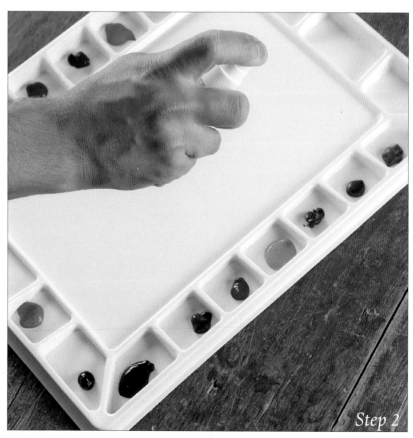

Step 2

3. Soak the sponge in clear water and wet your paper in a rectangular shape, as this will bring more water to the paper than a brush.

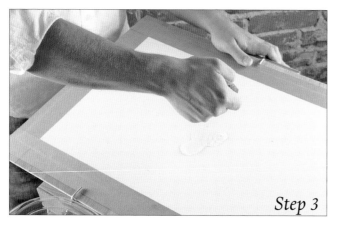

Step 3

4. Spread the water around, making certain all areas that will be painted on are wet.

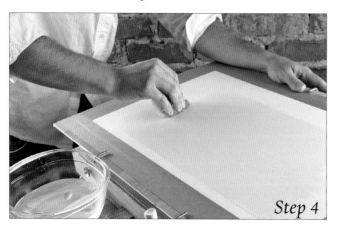

Step 4

5. Dip a 1" flat into clear water to soften the bristles. Load the brush with any color of paint from the palette.

6. Mix a few different colors in the palette's center section. *Notes: I prefer to mix colors toward the edge, near the side compartments. This allows for creating various blends of analogous colors, with greater ease. Remember, the colors you choose are not as important as noticing what the paint does when used.*

7. Stroke brush from side to side across the wet paper, and watch as the water pulls the paint from the bristles. *Note: Notice how the color grows lighter if paint is not reloaded.*

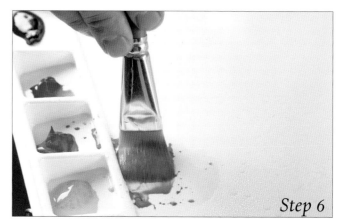

Step 6

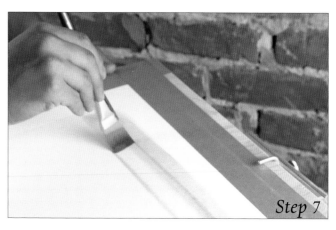

Step 7

8. For a wash to be successful, it is important the surface of the paper remain wet. To rewet the paper, mist the areas needing moisture with the spray bottle, or use the appropriately sized brush to stroke clear water in the desired areas.

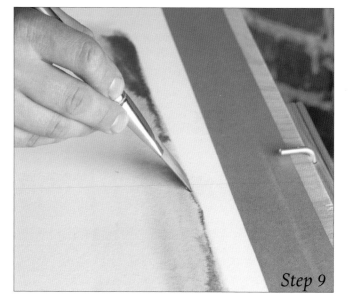

Step 9

9. Try using all of the brushes, and experiment with different ways to use each one. For example, try stroking the flat brush sideways. *Note: Remember, this wash exercise is not for painting a picture. Make brush strokes loose in order to resist making the wash exercise too tight or controlled.*

10. Introduce more colors to the paper, using the clean brush of your choice. It is important to achieve a smooth flowing transition between colors, which will not be possible if the paper dries. *Note: Think of the water on your paper as a road. The water in the paint is a vehicle, and the paint itself is a passenger. The vehicle cannot carry the passenger where there is no road.*

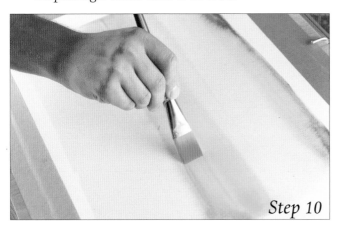

Step 10

11. Heavily load the brush of your choice with paint. Touch it to a wet area, and let the paint flow from the brush.

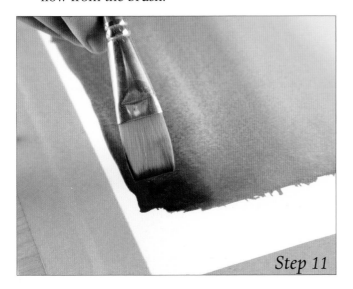

Step 11

Painting Removal

1. Allow the paper to dry, then use a craft knife to cut the tape holding the paper to the board. *Note: You can use your straightedge as a guide to cut lines straight.*

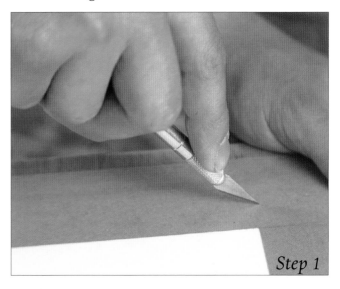

Step 1

2. Cut all four sides and lift the paper off. Trim off any tape still remaining on the edges.

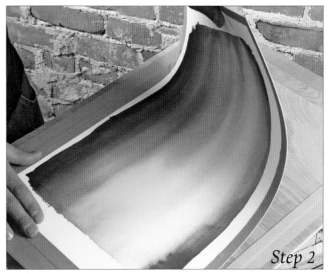

Step 2

Notes: This wash exercise has familiarized you with everything you need to know about how watercolor paints respond. It is a good idea to repeat this project several times in order to become comfortable with the way the paint works.

2
Technique

Materials:

- Brushes: #10 round, #14 round, ¹/₂" flat

- Clear water basin

- Craft knife or razor blade

- Eraser

- Paper towel

- Pencil

- Prepared watercolor palette (Refer to Palette Preparation on pages 14–15)

- Rinse water basin

- Sea sponge

- Spray bottle

- Watercolor paper, 15" x 22"

How do I paint using a controlled wash?

This technique differs from the basic wash in one important aspect: the outside perimeter of the wash will define a shape. In this exercise, we will paint a picture of seashells and a sea star. This subject contains some very simple shapes and interesting patterns.

One important thing to remember in this technique is that you are in control of the edges. Remember the road analogy in Step 10 on page 27. The paint will only travel where the paper is wet. You decide those limits, and where the paint will stop.

1. Tear and stretch your watercolor paper. Refer to Paper Stretching instructions on pages 16–17.

2. Transfer the image onto the watercolor paper. Refer to Image Transferring instructions on pages 20–21.

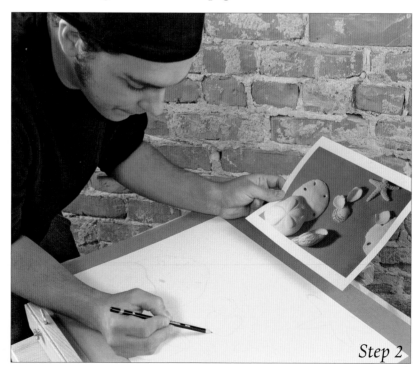

Step 2

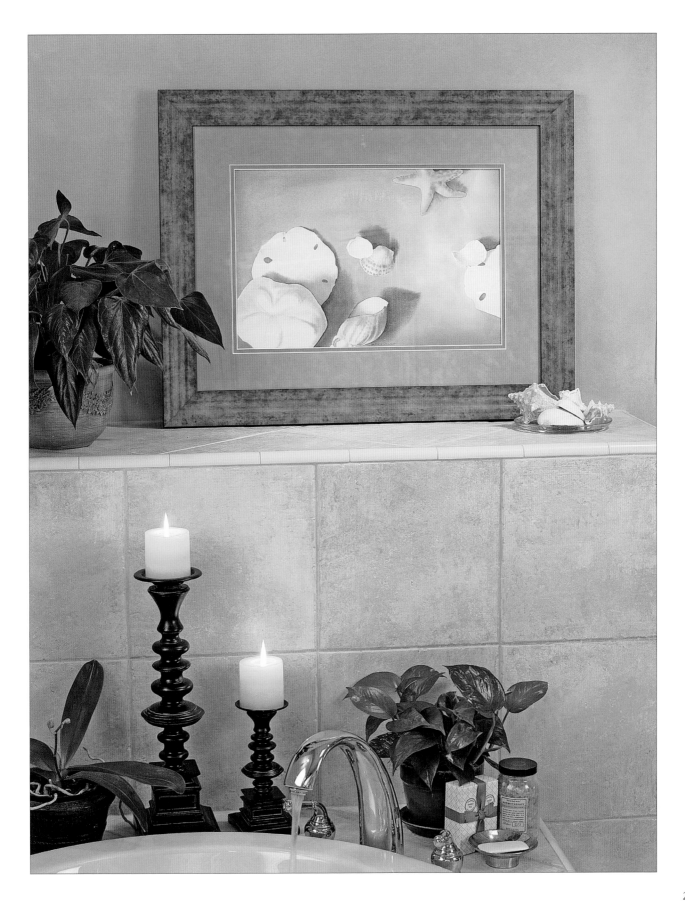

3. Mist the palette with the spray bottle.

4. Load the #14 round with clear water, and wet the background that lies between the seashells, tracing around the shapes. *Note: During this process, you may have to rewet areas to which water has already been applied; just to be certain that the entire area is wet when color is added.*

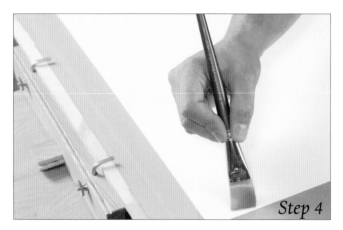

Step 4

5. Load the brush with Yellow Ochre. Mix the paint with enough water to ensure that it will carry across the wet paper.

6. Touch the paint to the wet background shape. *Note: The paint will easily leave the brush and flow onto the paper.*

7. Clean the brush in the rinse water. Wet any remaining dry spots within the shape with clear water. *Note: If the paint is not readily flowing from the bristles, add more water to the paint for a higher water to paint ratio. Any dry spots will become more apparent when touched with color.*

8. Make certain the color flows smoothly into all corners of the wet shape. The water might not diffuse the color as far as necessary, so use your brush to stroke the color to the far edges of the shape. Avoid attempting to make the shape an even tone, as some spots will remain more intense than others. *Note: This will ultimately add more interest to your work.*

9. Continuing with the #14 round, mix in a bit of Burnt Sienna with the Yellow Ochre and create

some slightly darker spots within the shape. *Note: Notice how the color stays inside the defined shape.*

I have chosen to leave the perimeter of my painting slightly darker, as you will notice in the finished piece.

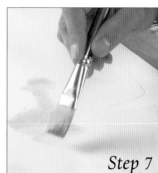

Step 5

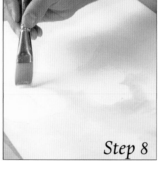

Step 7

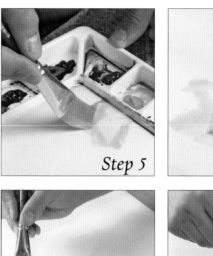

Step 8

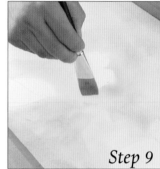

Step 9

10. Carefully soak up any excess water with a paper towel. Lightly dab the paper towel in the puddle, but do not wipe.

11. Rinse the brush, then mix a bit of Burnt Umber in with the Burnt Sienna and Yellow Ochre blend to deepen the color for the cast shadows. *Notes: Be certain not to add too much, though, or shadows may come out overwhelmingly heavy.*

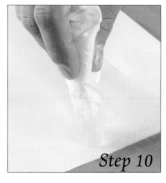

Step 10

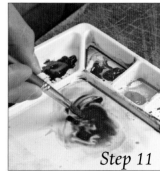

Step 11

If the paper becomes too dry at any point during the wash, simply apply more clear water with a clean brush, in order to keep it wet and workable.

12. Using the #10 round, loosely outline one side of each seashore shape with the colors already mixed to create shadows.

13. Define the shape of the cast shadow by lightly painting a perimeter for the area in which the shadow should fall. Fill in the shadow, allowing the paint to diffuse with only minimal guidance. Allow some areas to remain slightly lighter. *Note: Avoid making the shadow too large, as the paint will spread.*

14. Allow the paper to dry completely. *Note: If the paper is not completely dry, the wet areas will bleed together. Although this blending can be an attractive feature of watercolor paintings, it requires much skill and practice.*

15. Using the ½" flat, wash one of the sand dollars with clear water. *Note: Avoid allowing the water to seep outside the sand dollar lines, or the paint will flow outside as well.*

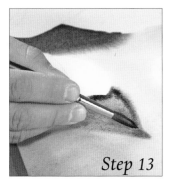

Step 13

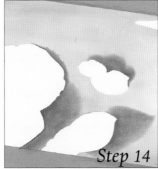

Step 14

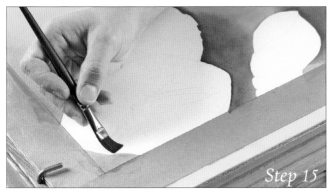

Step 15

16. Dilute a bit of Ultramarine Blue and a touch of Ivory Black with plenty of water. *Note: To create a tint, or lighter value of a color, add water. Instead of adding white paint, the white paper serves as all the white you need. The thinner the paint is, the more the white will show through, thus, making it lighter. Using the #10 round, paint in the shadow edge of the sand dollar. Notes: Keep in mind that this is the shadowed edge of a white object, so keep the shadow light.*

*A **cast shadow** is the term used for the shadow an object casts away from itself, onto another object.*

*The **shadow side** is the side of an object that is not directly hit by light, and therefore, is more shadowed.*

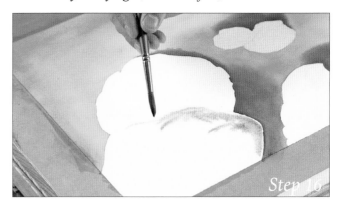

Step 16

17. Paint in oval strokes to imply the five-pointed bump on top of the sand dollar.

Note: The most important thing to consider is that you are not painting a sand dollar, rather, you are copying the shapes and colors. Concentrate on painting the colors where you see them, not on actually producing an image. Remember, everything you paint is simply a collection of shapes composed of different colors and values.

18. Paint the light, wet, blue-gray color onto the shape to establish broader shadows. *Note: Do not move on to paint the sand dollar adjacent to the first, as the colors will bleed together and the shapes will be lost. Always move on to a part of the painting that does not touch the wet part in order to maintain crisp edges.*

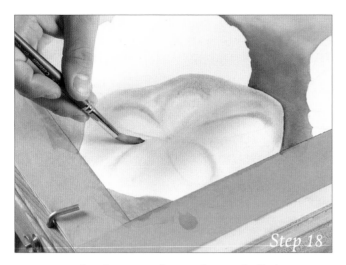

19. Using the #10 round, wet the seashell shape in the center of the painting with clear water. Touch in a bit of Yellow Ochre at the edges of the shell.

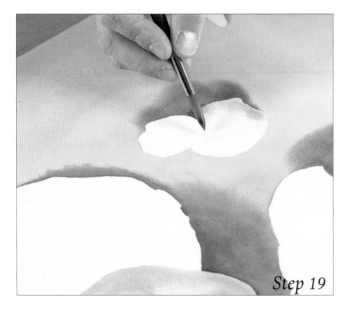

Step 19

20. Add some Yellow Ochre to a little of the blue-gray mixture used on the sand dollar. Lightly dab the paint onto the shadow side to give the shell some form.

21. Use the #4 round to paint an arch of Cadmium Yellow across the shell. This creates a background where the pattern will be painted later on.

22. Continuing with the #4 round, paint some gray "stripes" which will indicate the ridges of the

seashell. *Notes: We do this after the yellow arch in order to pull some of the yellow into the stripes, which will then add the illusion of the shapes having ridges.*

There are several stages of drying that your wet paper goes through. First, when the area is very wet, the paint will disperse rather evenly. As the paper dries, the stroke's detail is more retained. You will begin to get a feel for how long to wait in order to produce strokes with different levels of clarity.

23. Remove any puddles, as the paper will accept much more paint. *Note: If the paint is floating in a puddle of water, you have less control over where it "lands."*

24. Allow the paper to dry. Using the #4 round, dab in the reddish-orange spots. Create a light mixture Yellow Ochre and Cadmium Red, and dab the color onto the shell.

25. Add a little Burnt Sienna, and continue along the yellow arch.

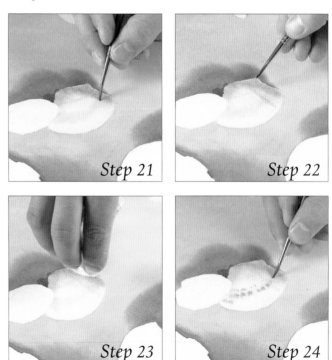

Step 21

Step 22

Step 23

Step 24

26. Following the same pattern, create two or three more rows of spots. Keep them somewhat random-looking.

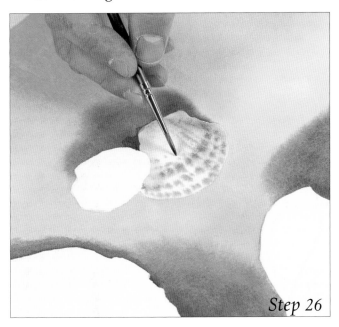

Step 26

27. Continuing with the #4 round, go back through the shell, touching in some yellows and reds, and even a little violet, until the desired look is achieved. *Note: Be careful not to overwork the painting, or it may appear muddy.*

28. Wet the sea star with clear water, using the #4 round. Cover it in a wash using the same Yellow Ochre and Burnt Sienna mixture applied to the background. Add more Burnt Sienna, and dab in the darker spots of color by applying the same method used for the reddish seashell.

29. Paint the remaining sand dollars and seashells in the same manner as those already painted.

30. Allow the painting to dry thoroughly, and then cut it off the plywood board. Refer to Painting Removal instructions on page 27. Sign your painting.

Note: Look at the model photograph on page 29 and notice that all of the shells, sand dollars, and the sea star are simple, basic washes, with no added detail

after drying. The second dollar uses the same technique as the first, as the cast shadow is the same as the shadows on the background shape. The sea star is done in almost the same colors as the background, but has some richer spots touched in. The seashell at the bottom is composed of two separate washes: one blue-gray wash for the inside, and colored stripes added after the blue-gray has dried.

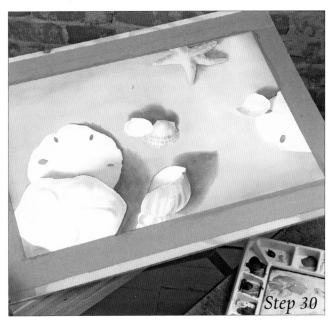

Step 30

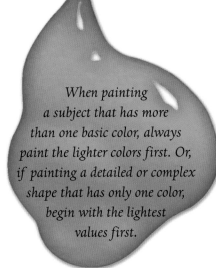

When painting a subject that has more than one basic color, always paint the lighter colors first. Or, if painting a detailed or complex shape that has only one color, begin with the lightest values first.

3

Technique

Materials:

- Brushes: #1 round, #4 round, #10 round, #14 round, 1/2" flat, 1" flat

- Clear water basin

- Craft knife or razor blade

- Eraser

- Paper towel

- Pencil

- Prepared watercolor palette (Refer to Palette Preparation on pages 14–15)

- Rinse water basin

- Sea sponge

- Spray bottle

- Watercolor paper, 15" x 22"

How do I add detail to my painting?

Now that you have mastered the basic and controlled washes, you are ready to add some fine detail to your work. The main difference between adding detail and painting a wash is that we do not begin by wetting the paper with clear water first. Rather, we begin with a paint-loaded brush. Generally, detail is painted over the top of a thoroughly dried wash.

1. Tear and stretch the watercolor paper. Refer to Paper Stretching instructions on pages 16–17.

2. Transfer the image onto the paper. Refer to Image Transferring instructions on pages 20–21.

3. Using the spray bottle, mist the paper with water.

4. Using the 1" flat, create a smooth, soft, extremely subtle wash with a light blue at the top of the paper and a light, golden brown at the bottom. Allow the painting to dry completely.

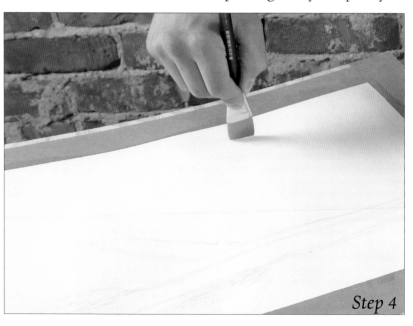

Step 4

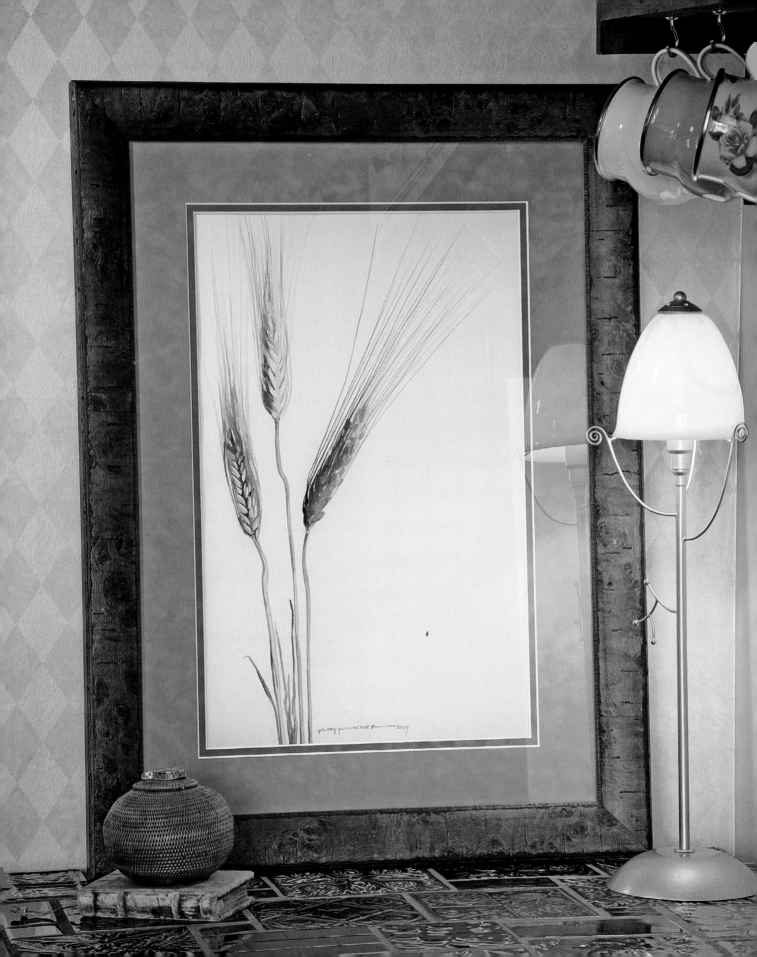

5. Next, load the #4 round with a light wet mixture of Yellow Ochre and Burnt Sienna. Stroke the shapes of the wheat heads.

6. Using the #1 round, stroke the long stems with a slightly richer tone of the same hue. Keep the lines thin and smooth.

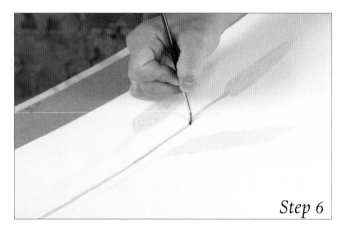

Step 6

7. Go over the stems again with a darker color, if needed.

Note: This technique requires less drying time, as the paper is not painted with water first.

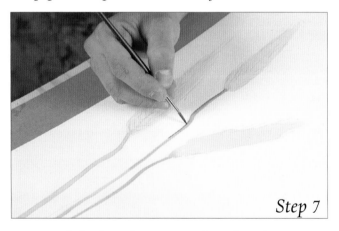

Step 7

8. Switch back to the #4 round, and apply a suggestion of a shadow edge along wheat stem.

9. With your brush still loaded with the richer Yellow Ochre and Burnt Sienna blend, create some thin, grassy extensions near the bottom. Follow the same pattern as stems, beginning light and building to the darker values.

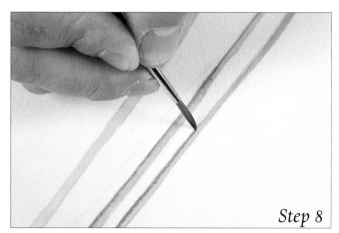

Step 8

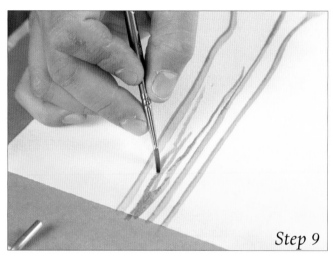

Step 9

Notes: Now you are ready to paint the wheat heads. Although the details may seem intimidating, when broken down into several layers, it is not nearly as complex as it may appear.

Notice the difference between this technique and painting a wash. Every stroke remains visible on this painting, and nothing will bleed into the background unless it is still wet.

10. Define the seed shapes.

11. Continue with seed shapes through to the tip.

12. Using the same color and the #1 round, pull away from the shape to create the grassy points. *Note: Small brushes do not hold much water or paint, so the brush should run dry after each stroke. This will automatically create a nice fade, and a sharp end of the grass extensions.*

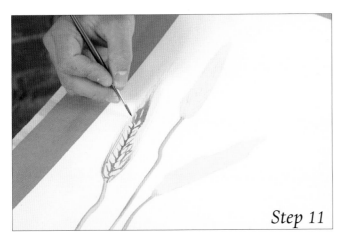

Step 11

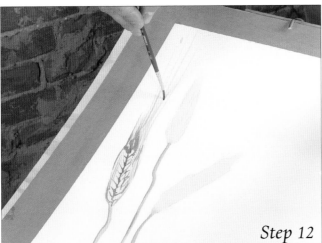

Step 12

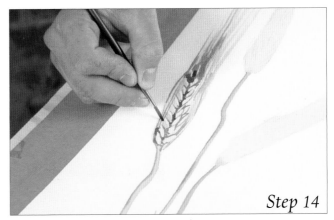

Step 14

15. The last color applied will be nearly black. Use this sparingly, as you will need very little of this dark rich color to darken the entire shape. *Note: Once such a dark color has been applied, there is no turning back. Be careful to avoid covering up other details and colors.*

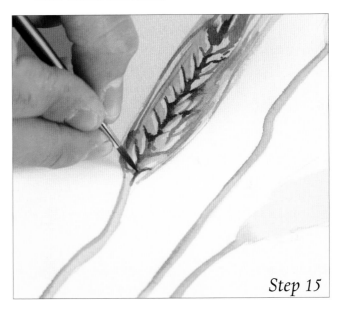

Step 15

13. Come back through the wheat head and add a slightly darker color. To avoid graying, mix in some Burnt Umber. *Note: If you use black to create your darker shades, the colors will have a tendency to appear gray. To avoid this, try using blues and browns where you can to keep the paints looking rich and fresh.*

14. Build your shadows from light to dark, slowly adding more detail and deeper shadows. At this point, you may want to load your brush with clear water and paint in some light shadows across the shapes to leave some slight highlights. *Note: The clear water will pick up just enough of the colors on the paper to leave some vivid highlights in between.*

16. Allow the painting to dry thoroughly, then cut it off the plywood board. Refer to Painting Removal instructions on page 27. Sign your painting.

Note: Detail can be added in this fashion over very simple washes such as this one, or over far more complex washes. This technique is what will give pictures the "punch" that will set them apart from other watercolor paintings.

4
Technique

Materials:

- Art tape

- Brushes: #1 round, #4 round, #10 round, #14 round, $\frac{1}{2}$" flat, 1" flat

- Clear water basin

- Craft knife or razor blade

- Eraser

- Paper towel

- Pencil

- Prepared watercolor palette (Refer to Palette Preparation on pages 14–15)

- Rinse water basin

- Sea sponge

- Spray bottle

- Watercolor paper, 15" x 22"

How do I combine detail with a controlled wash?

This exercise will cover the basic wash learned in Technique One on pages 24–27, the controlled wash learned in Technique Two on pages 28–33, and adding detail as covered in Technique Three on pages 34–37. For this piece, we will not use an entire stretched half-sheet of paper, but will instead tape off a rectangular area of the desired size.

1. Tear and stretch your watercolor paper. Refer to Paper Stretching instructions on pages 16–17.

2. Transfer the image onto paper. Refer to Image Transferring instructions on pages 20–21.

3. Tape off the area surrounding the image using art tape.

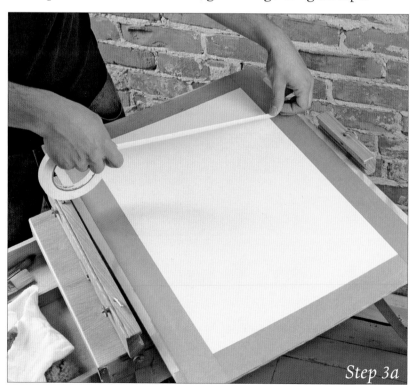

Step 3a

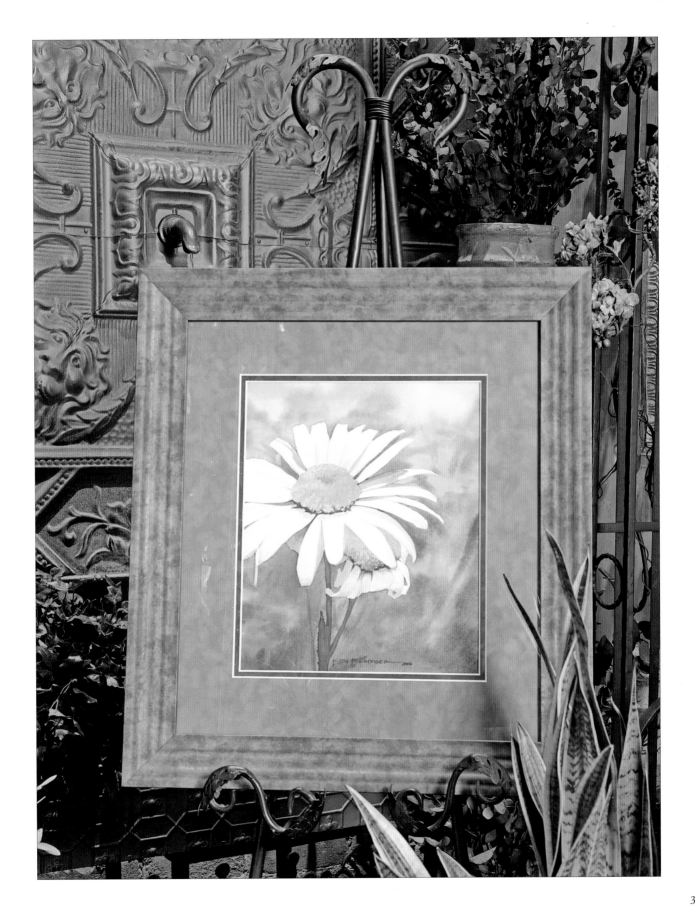

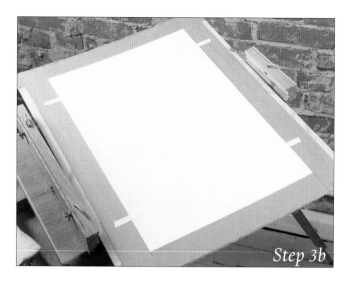

Step 3b

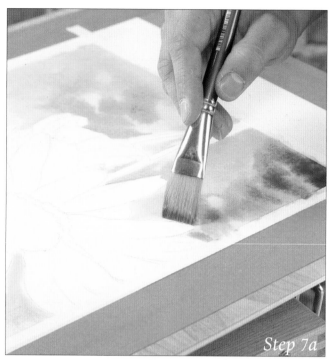

Step 7a

4. Wet the background shape with the 1" flat dipped in clear water, as covered in Step 4 for Technique Two on pages 28-33.

5. Still using the 1" flat, wash the background with multiple hues of green, yellow, and blue. Begin with the lighter colors.

6. Lay down a layer of light blues, then touch in some yellow.

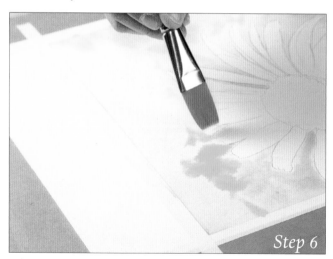

Step 6

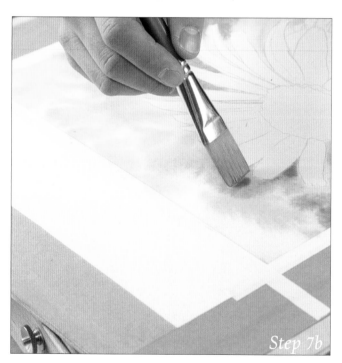

Step 7b

7. Continue by touching in various greens.

Note: As with the sand dollar in Step 16 on page 31, since the main foreground color is white, the darker wash in the background will define your shapes. Keep this in mind as you paint around the perimeter of what will later become the flower petals.

Note: Although this might look like a blurry mess now, the finished piece will look like flowers and plants in the distance. This is because your mind assumes that's what it is. Your imagination will fill in, even with only a suggestion of shape.

8. Load the #10 round with clear water. Allow a few water droplets to drip into the wash on the painting. *Note: This is what I call "chasing." The water will "chase" the color outward by creating a lighter spot. This is a valuable tool for making random blurry highlights in an ambiguous background.*

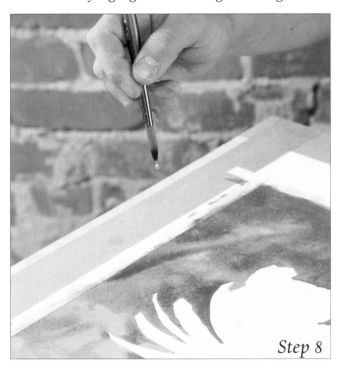

Step 8

9. Lightly dab in other subtle colors to add interest. *Note: Keep the overall tone of the background fairly dark to better "lift" the foreground or subject off the page. Allow the painting to dry completely.*

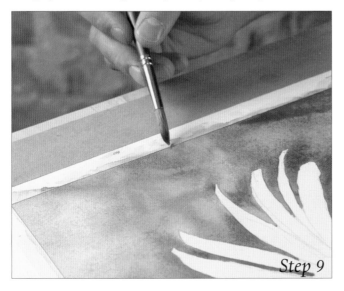

Step 9

10. To add detail, fill the #14 round with dark green paint and stroke the stems of the flower the same as the stems of wheat. *Note: Remember, this is a wet-on-dry technique, which will not work unless the paper is dry.*

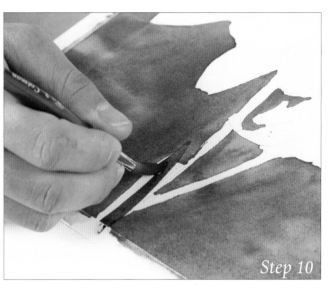

Step 10

11. Paint the tops of the stems, using the #10 round. *Note: This is what will define the shapes of the petals-to-be.*

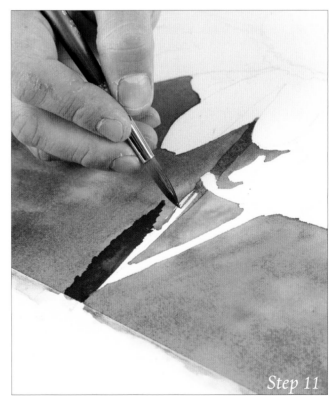

Step 11

12. Continuing with the #10 round, skip to an area that is not adjacent to the wet section. Create a soft yellow wash within the center of each flower, making one edge slightly darker for shape.

13. Add a bit of yellow-green to the base of the center washes.

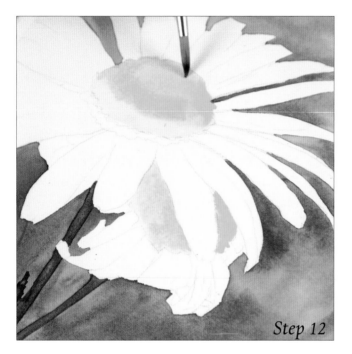

Step 12

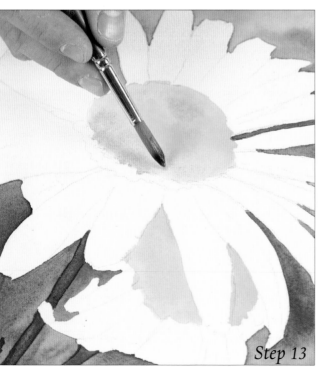

Step 13

14. Allow the center washes to dry.

15. Rinse the #10 round, and switch to a very light blue-gray to wash each petal individually.

16. Wet each petal with clear water and lightly touch in shadows. *Note: Don't worry about the shadows mixing together, as detail will be added later which will separate them.*

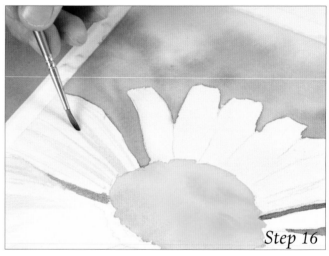

Step 16

17. As the petals become drier, begin adding in detail with the #4 round.

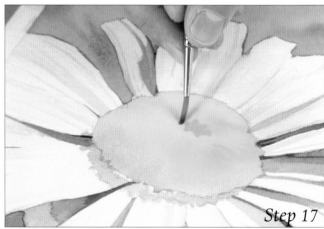

Step 17

18. Let the small washes dry before painting in the cast shadows to ensure a crisp edge. Repeat this process for the lower flower.

19. While the petals dry, begin adding detail to the center. Start with a darker yellow spot in the middle.

20. Apply small, random strokes of a grayed mixture of yellow-green to imply the texture.

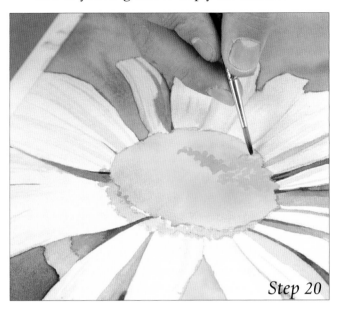

Step 20

21. Use a slightly darker color around the bottom edge.

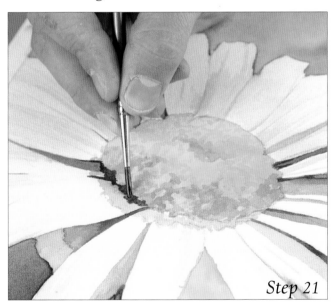

Step 21

22. Using the darkest green mixture, add the final details, which will define the shape and finish off the flower. Allow to dry thoroughly.

23. Finish the lower flower in the same manner.

24. Peel up the tape carefully so the paper does not tear.

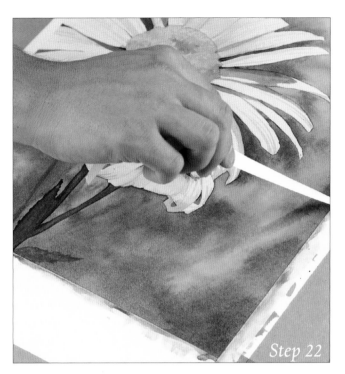

Step 22

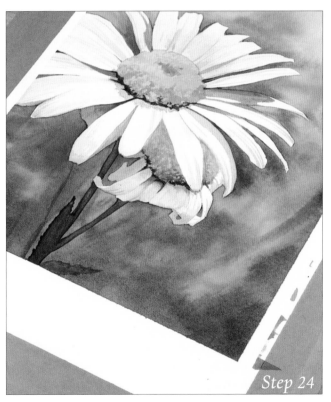

Step 24

25. Allow the painting to dry thoroughly, then cut it off the plywood board. Refer to Painting Removal instructions on page 27. Sign your painting.

5
Technique

Materials:

- Brushes: #1 round, $\frac{1}{2}$" flat

- Clear water basin

- Craft knife or razor blade

- Eraser

- Paper towel

- Pencil

- Prepared watercolor palette
  (Refer to Palette
  Preparation on pages 14–15)

- Rinse water basin

- Sea sponge

- Spray bottle

- Toothbrush

- Watercolor paper,
  15" x 22"

How do I use the spattering technique?

This exercise consists of simple geometric shapes. There are many manmade shapes available to use as subject matter if you are more comfortable with them than with organic matter such as seashells and flowers. One such example is architecture, or more specifically, architectural features.

Spattering is a simple technique that is not much more complex than it sounds. However, there is a bit of a trick to it.

1. Tear and stretch your watercolor paper. Refer to Paper Stretching instructions on pages 16–17.

2. Transfer the image onto paper. Refer to Image Transferring instructions on pages 20–21.

3. Using the $\frac{1}{2}$" flat, wash every other horizontal "band" of stone, beginning with the topmost stripe.

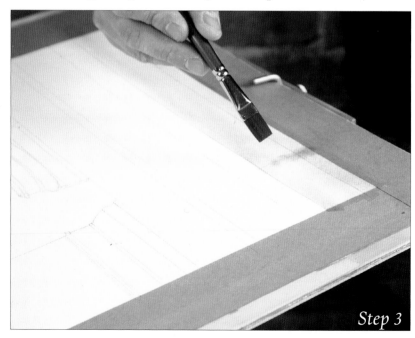

Step 3

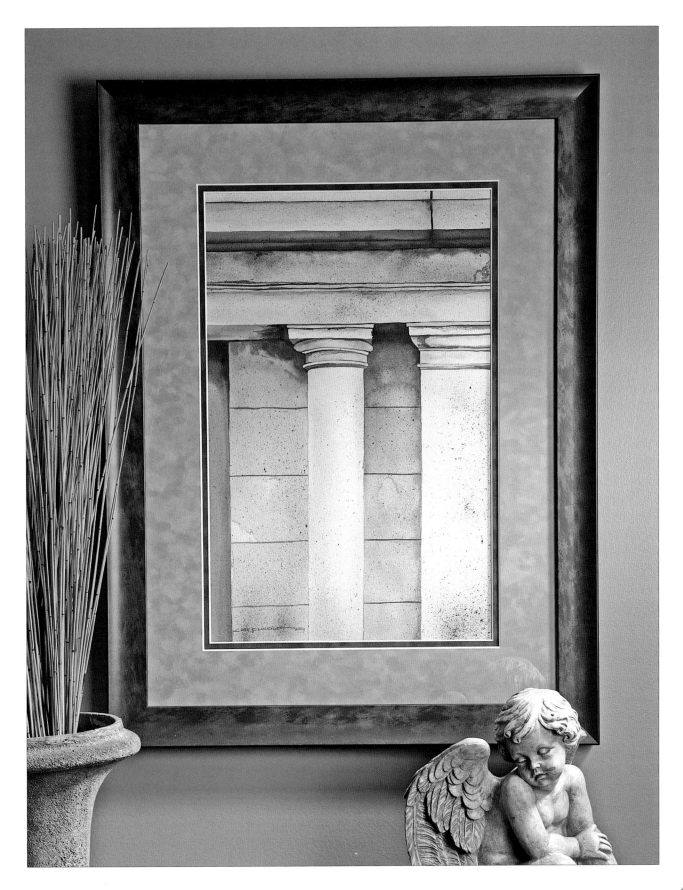

4. To make the stone "breathe," or appear more lively, avoid limiting your palette with those colors generally associated with stone, like blues and grays. Incorporate warmer tones such as reds, browns, Burnt Sienna, and Burnt Umber.

5. Continue this process with each shape, allowing the columns themselves to add soft detail. *Note: Painting shapes in areas that are not adjacent to the ones drying will, again, allow you to keep working while the wet shapes dry.*

6. While the areas already painted dry, go back between them to paint the remaining stone.

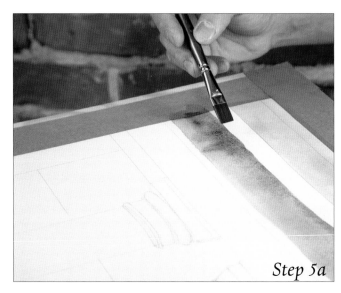

Step 5a

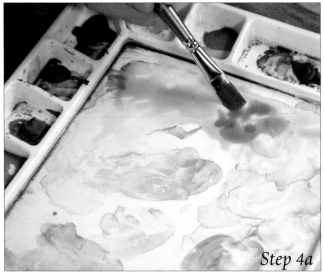

Step 4a

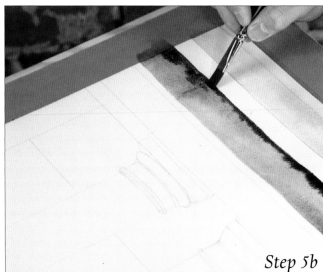

Step 5b

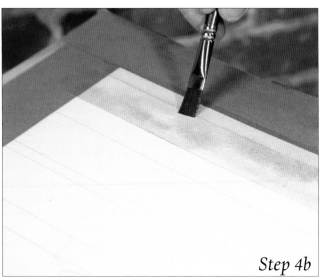

Step 4b

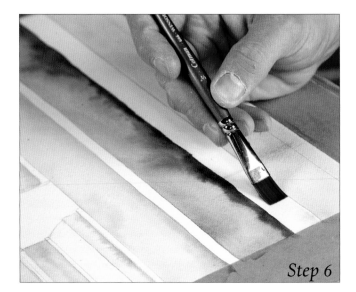

Step 6

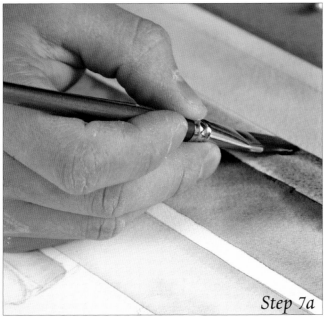

Step 7a

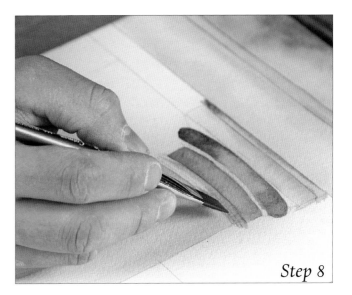

Step 8

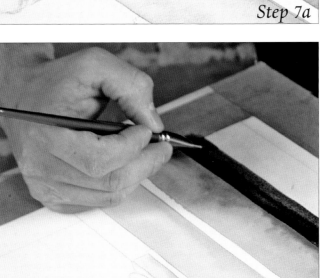

Step 7b

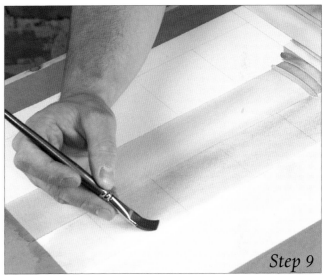

Step 9

7. For the darker bands, build up value from lighter colors.

8. Finish the horizontal banding on the pillars.

9. If the columns have dried thoroughly, wash the area between them with a slightly darker, warmer mixture of the same colors used for the rest of the painting. Be sure to maintain clean, sharp, straight edges.

10. Build up the dark values at the top for depth.

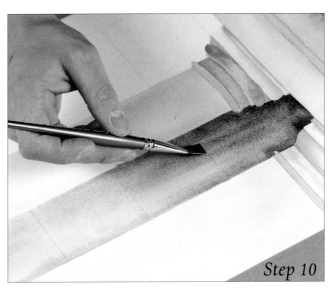

Step 10

11. To create some interest in the texture of the stone, use a clean paper towel to dab some of the color and water as it dries. Press the paper towel down harder than when lifting unwanted puddles, as the idea is to create a deliberate dry spot. *Note: This will cause the wash to dry unevenly, adding interesting edges.*

12. Use the #1 round and a dark blue, almost black, mixture of paint to begin adding detail between and within the shapes. *Note: Be certain to paint on dry paper, or the paint will bleed too much.*

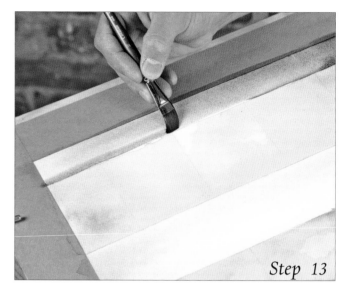

Step 13

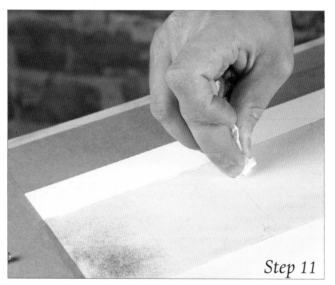

Step 11

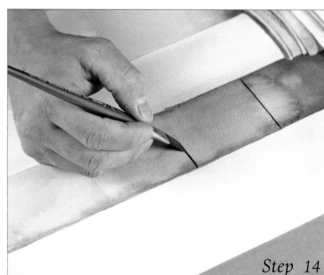

Step 14

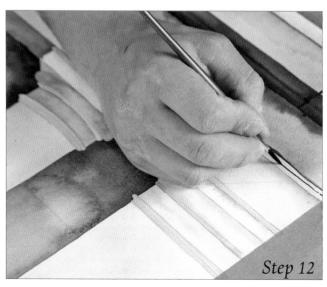

Step 12

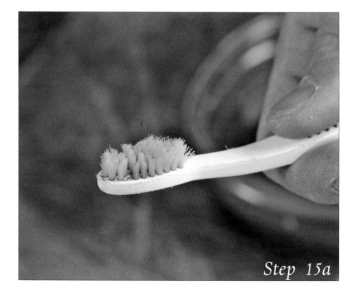

Step 15a

13. Wash the final large shape with a dark tan color, which will cause it to visually recede into the background. Allow to dry thoroughly.

14. Add the cracks on the flat face of the structure.

15. To spatter, use the toothbrush with trimmed bristles. Load the toothbrush with very wet, dark gray-brown paint.

16. Aim the tip of the brush at the part of the painting you want effected and drag your thumb across the bristles toward yourself.

17. To spatter more heavily in certain areas, create a mask with your hand. *Note: This will create a stone-like texture to add the finishing touch to the architectural rendering.*

18. Allow the painting to dry thoroughly, and then cut it off the plywood board. Refer to Painting Removal instructions on page 27. Sign your painting.

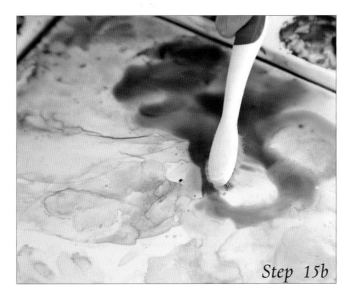

Step 15b

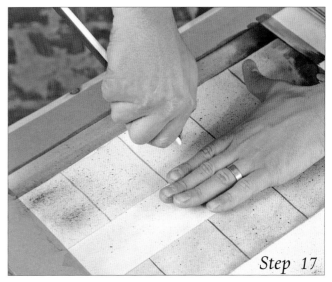

Step 17

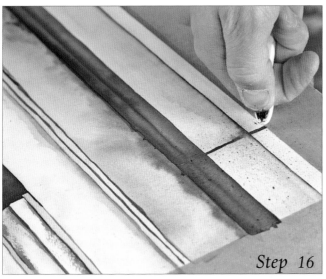

Step 16

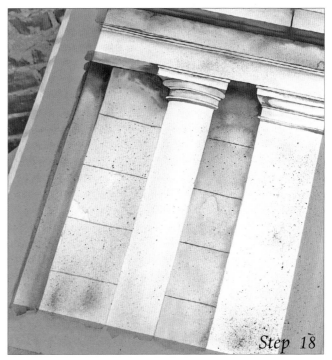

Step 18

6
Technique

Materials:

- Brush, 1" flat

- Clear water basin

- Craft knife or razor blade

- Disposable brush

- Eraser

- Liquid masking fluid
  Note: Liquid masking fluid will ruin your brush. Use one that can be discarded.

- Paper towel

- Pencil

- Prepared watercolor palette (Refer to Palette Preparation on pages 14–15)

- Rinse water basin

- Sea sponge

- Spray bottle

- Watercolor paper, 4" x 6"

How do I use the masking technique?

Masking is a useful technique for preserving crisp white spots while painting large washes. The advantage of masking is that you don't have to outline the white areas with paint. This allows for a smoother wash, without the buildup edge that occurs when painting around a subject.

For this exercise, we will create a postcard painting. Ready-made watercolor postcard tablets are available in most art supply stores, or you can cut watercolor paper to the standard 4" x 6" postcard size. Use at least 140 lb. paper to ensure that it is thick enough for postal delivery.

1. Tear and stretch your watercolor paper. Refer to Paper Stretching instructions on pages 16–17.

2. Transfer the image onto the paper. Refer to Image Transferring instructions on pages 20–21.

3. Paint the masking fluid onto the paper in the shape you want to mask, as though you were actually using paint. *Note: Shown here is a dragonfly silhouette.* Allow to dry thoroughly.

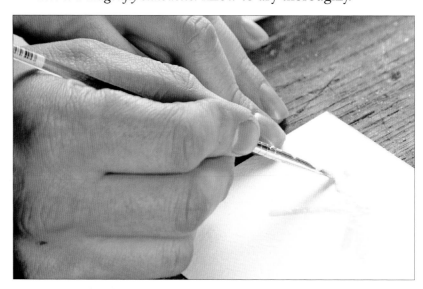

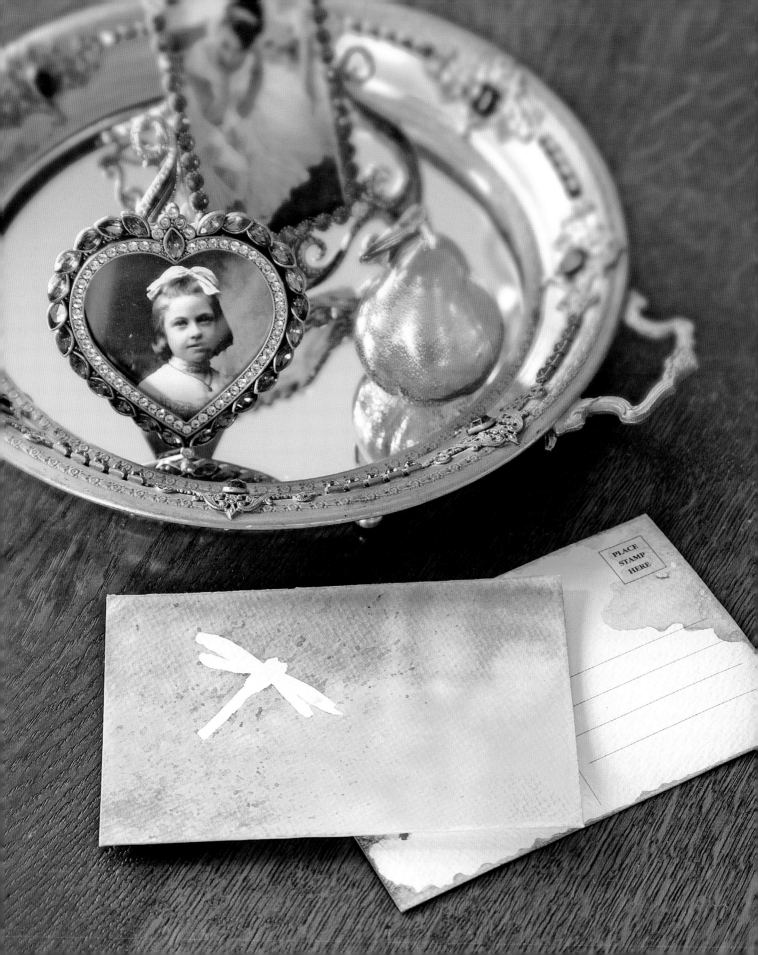

4. Place a dollop of masking fluid onto the palette lid or a scrap of paper. Set aside and allow to dry thoroughly.

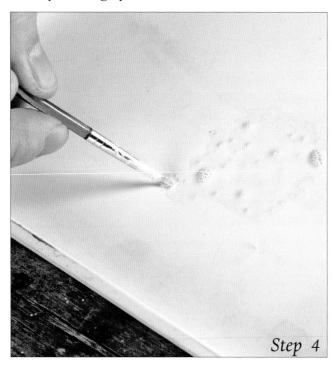

Step 4

5. Spray card with water to prepare it for the wash.

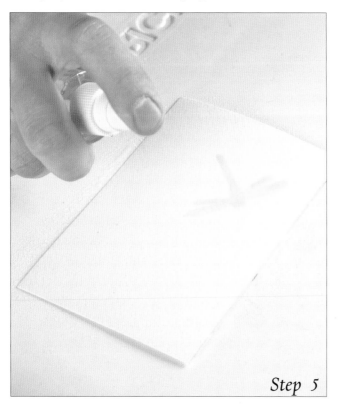

Step 5

6. Begin adding colors. *Note: Although you can use any color you like, I started out with a little Green Gold.*

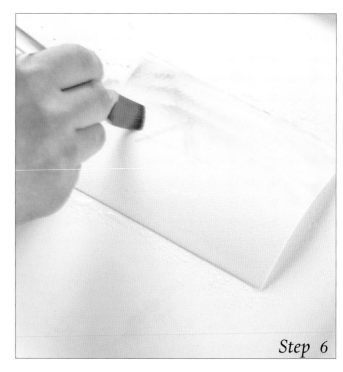

Step 6

7. Continue adding colors. Refer to Step 6 of Technique One, on page 26. *Note: I used Yellow Ochre, Burnt Sienna, Hooker's Green, and Raw Umber for my postcard.*

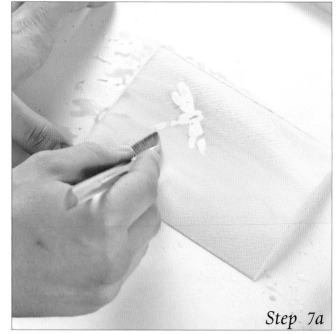

Step 7a

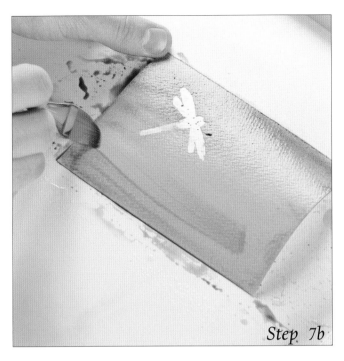

Step 7b

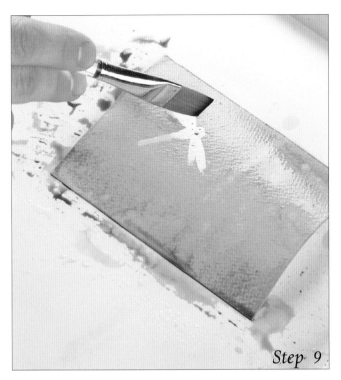

Step 9

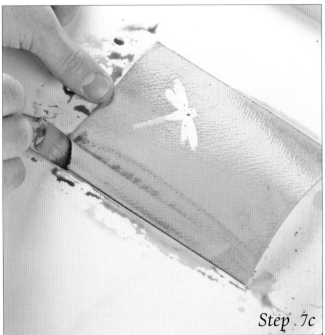

Step 7c

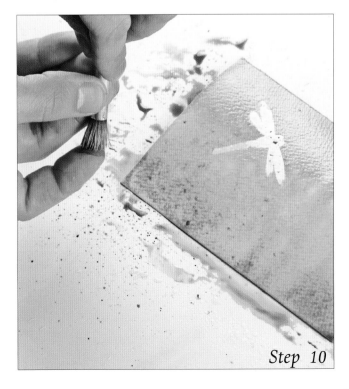

Step 10

8. Create some random "natural" effects by employing chasing. Refer to Step 8 in Technique Four, on page 41.

9. Load the brush with clear water, and "flip" it onto the painting by flicking the brush toward the paper. *Note: As we saw before with the chasing, this will dilute the paint, leaving some lighter spots.*

10. Using the 1" flat instead of the toothbrush, spatter some darker brown and green across the postcard while the wash is wet. Refer to Steps 15–17 Technique Five on page 49. Allow to dry thoroughly.

11. Repeat spattering with the same colors previously used. Allow to dry thoroughly.

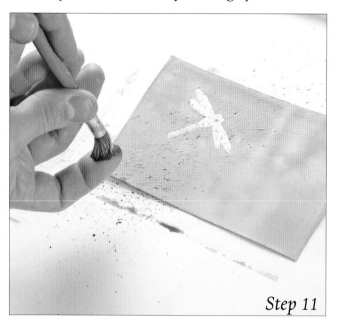

Step 11

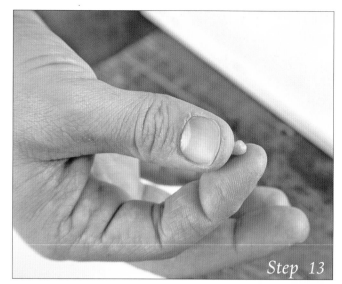

Step 13

12. Peel up the extra dollop of masking fluid that was previously placed on palette lid or paper scrap.

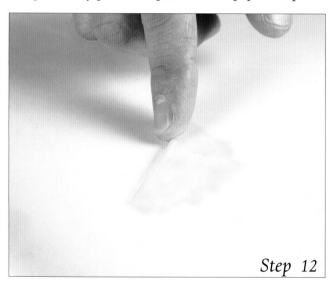

Step 12

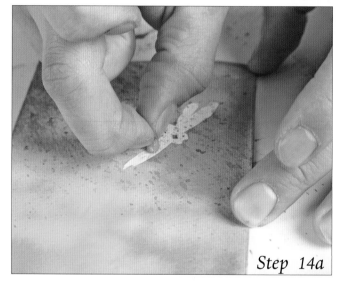

Step 14a

13. Roll it into a ball, which will then act as your masking fluid remover. *Note: There are also masking fluid/rubber cement removers available for purchase, as an alternative.*

14. Use mask remover to carefully pull up the mask. *Note: The mask will oftentimes stretch and peel off as one large piece.*

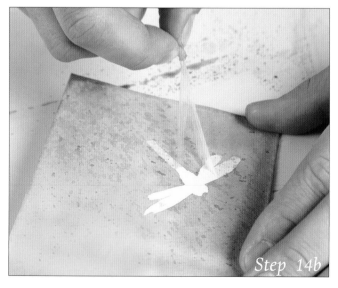

Step 14b

15. Allow the painting to dry thoroughly, then cut it off the plywood board. Refer to Painting Removal instructions on page 27. Sign your painting.

16. Now your postcard is ready to mail.

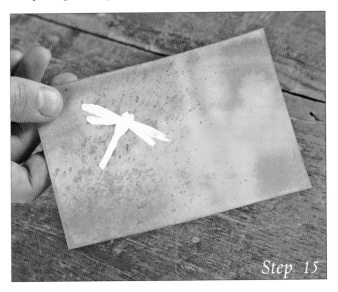

Step 15

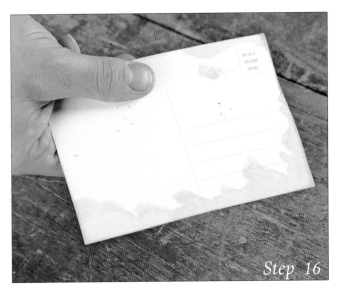

Step 16

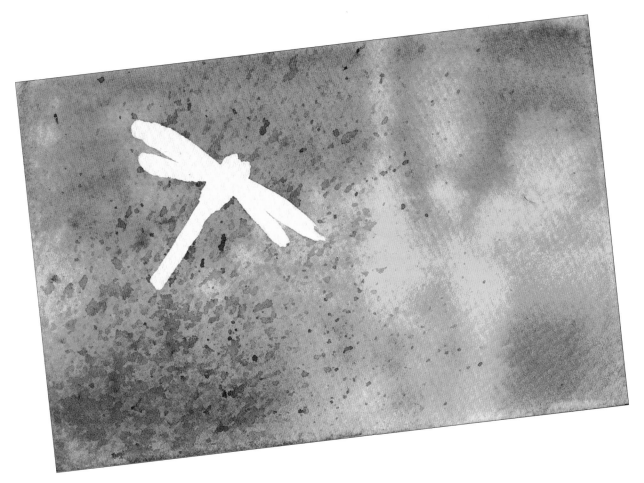

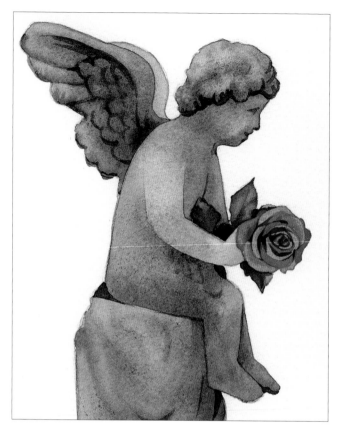

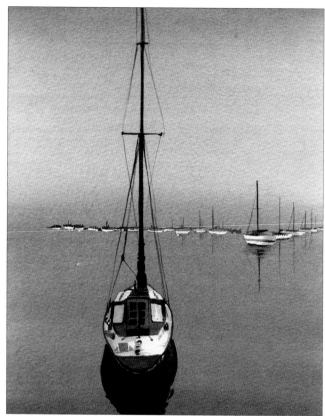

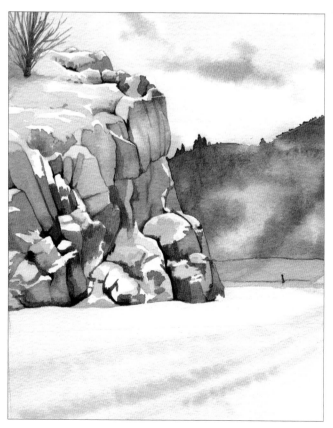

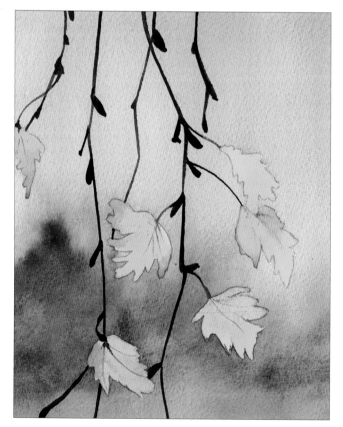

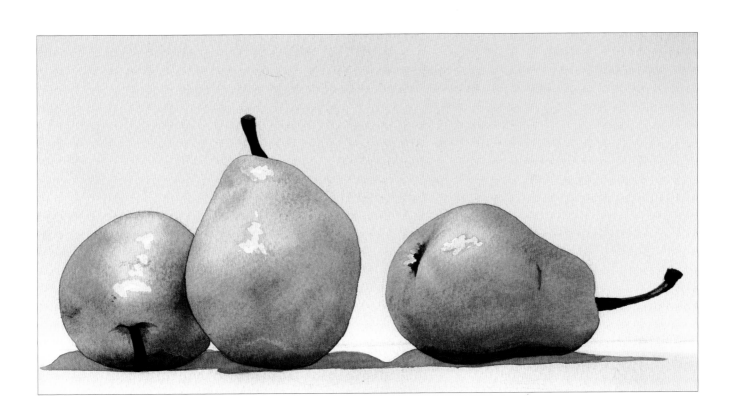

Section 3: *Beyond the Basics*

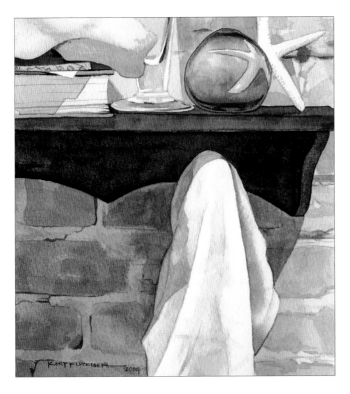

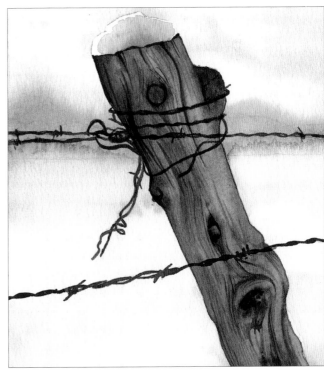

1
Project

Materials:

- Brushes: #1 round, #4 round, 1" flat

- Clear water basin

- Craft knife or razor blade

- Disposable brush

- Eraser

- Liquid masking fluid

- Paper towel

- Pencil

- Prepared watercolor palette (Refer to Palette Preparation on pages 14–15)

- Rinse water basin

- Sea sponge

- Spray bottle

- Watercolor paper, 15" x 22"

How do I paint within a masked area?

1. Tear and stretch your watercolor paper. Refer to Paper Stretching instructions on pages 16–17.

2. Transfer the image onto the paper. Refer to Image Transferring instructions on pages 20–21.

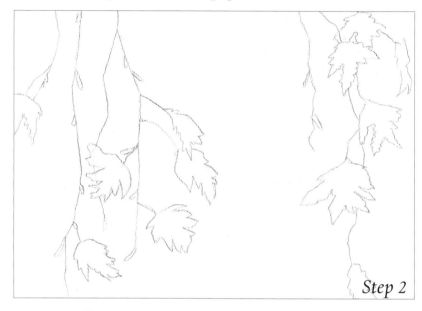

Step 2

3. Mask off the leaves. Refer to masking instructions in Steps 3–4 for Technique Six on pages 50–52.

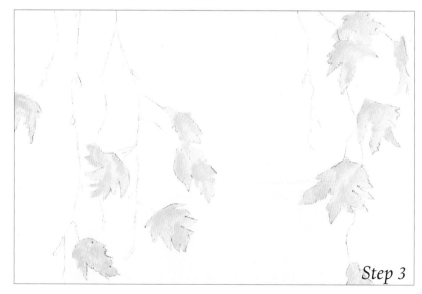

Step 3

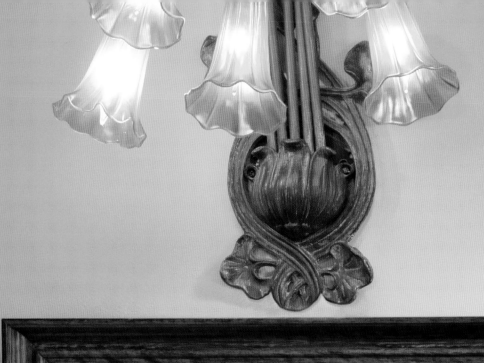
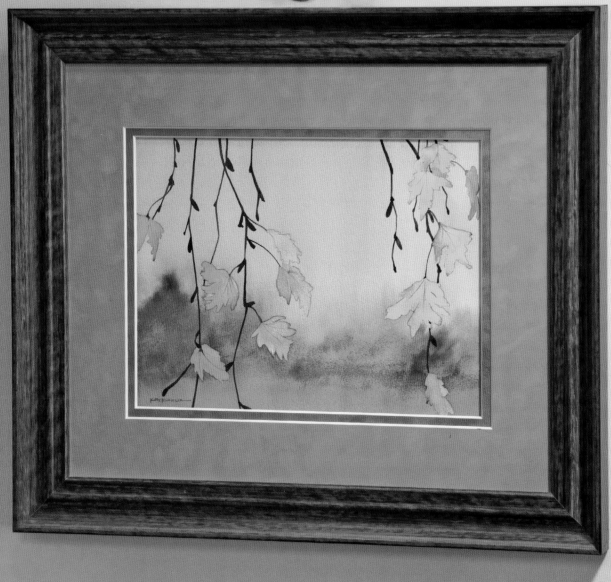

4. Apply the background wash, using the 1" flat. Refer to Technique One on pages 24–27. Allow to dry thoroughly.

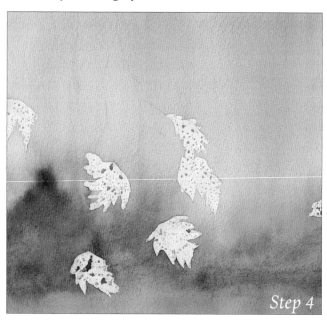
Step 4

5. Peel the masking off. Refer to masking instructions in Steps 11–12 for Technique Six.

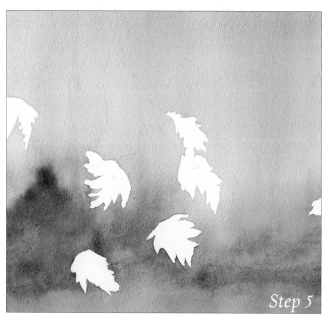
Step 5

6. Using the #4 round, apply a controlled wash within the leaves. Refer to Technique Two on pages 28–33. Add in detail.

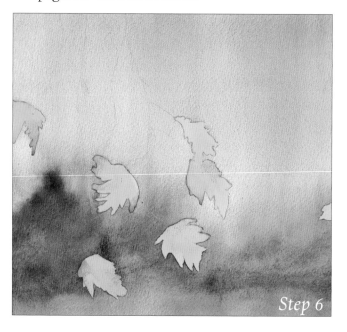
Step 6

7. Paint the branches with a dark burnt Umber. Alternate between the #4 round and the #1 round for varying degrees of detail.

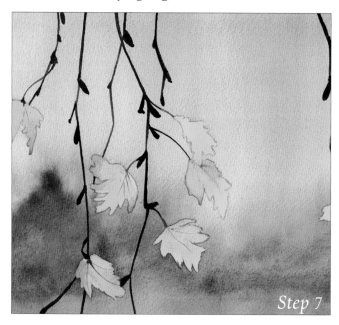
Step 7

8. Allow the painting to dry thoroughly, then cut it off the plywood board. Refer to Painting Removal instructions on page 27. Sign your painting.

How do I make a black-and-white painting?

To paint a black-and-white picture in watercolor, simply limit your palette to Ivory Black. Altering the water to paint ratios will offer an unlimited range of value.

1. Tear and stretch your watercolor paper. Refer to Paper Stretching instructions on pages 16–17.

2. Transfer the image onto the paper. Refer to Image Transferring instructions on pages 20–21.

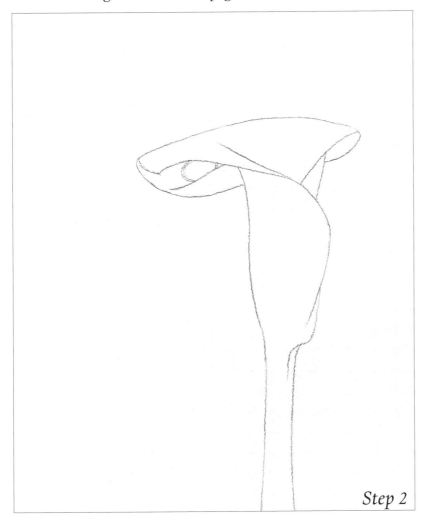

Step 2

2 Project

Materials:

- Brushes: #1 round, #4 round

- Clear water basin

- Craft knife or razor blade

- Eraser

- Paper towel

- Pencil

- Prepared watercolor palette (Refer to Palette Preparation on pages 14–15)

- Rinse water basin

- Sea sponge

- Spray bottle

- Watercolor paper, 15" x 22"

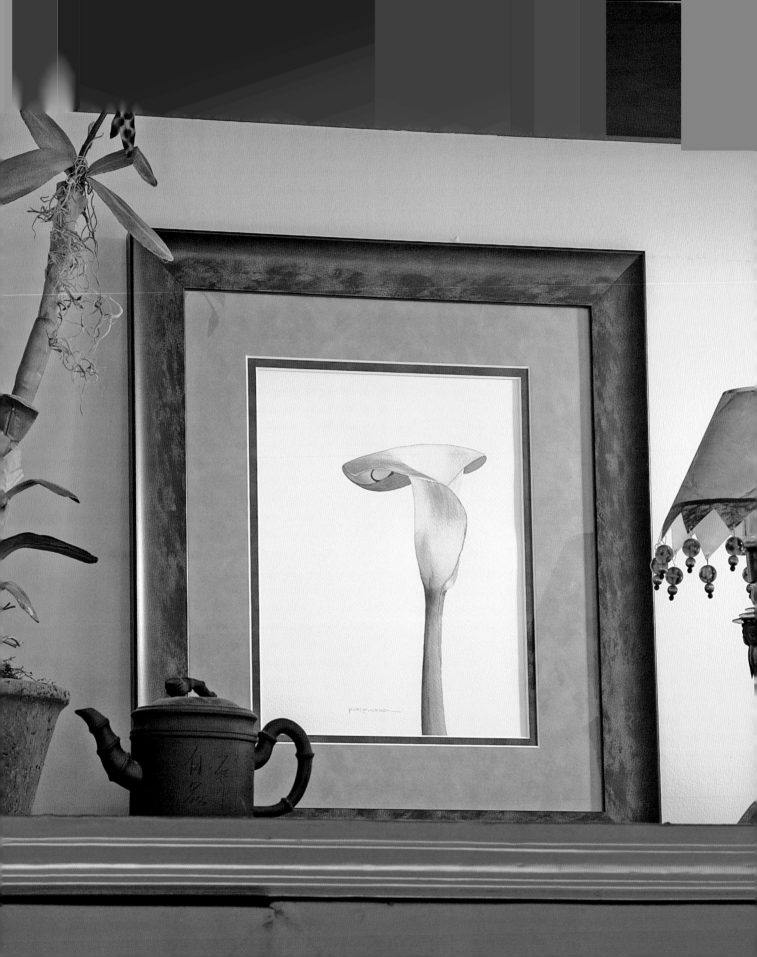

3. Using the #4 round, apply a series of controlled washes, taking the picture one shape at a time. Refer to Technique Two on pages 28–33.

4. Leave the slight white edge along the bottom of the first shape.

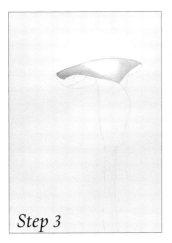
Step 3

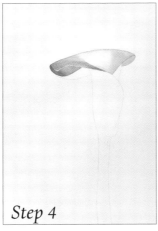
Step 4

5. Alternating between the #1 round and #4 round for varying degrees of detail, add the darker underfold of the calla lily petal, then the lighter side. Wait for each shape to dry completely before moving on to the next. Allow painting to dry thoroughly.

6. Using the #1 round, add the dark curl inside the petal fold. Refer to Steps 6–7 for Technique 3 on page 36.

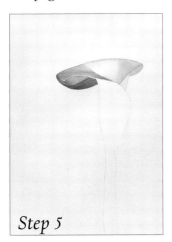
Step 5

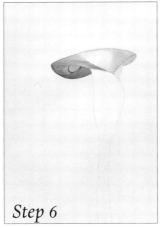
Step 6

7. *Note: In order to have a soft transition between the petal and the stem without creating unwanted lines, the next shape must be done as one complete wash.* Wet the entire shape with clear water before applying the paint. Using the #4 round, leave some lighter soft strokes visible on the side of the petal.

8. Finish the right side of the petal with a light wash and stroke in some bands of darker gray on the shade side of the flower, leaving the lighter stripes visible.

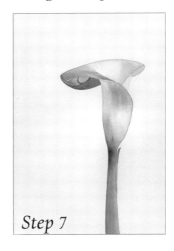
Step 7

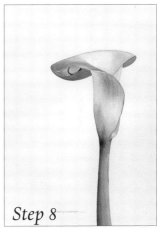
Step 8

9. Allow the painting to dry thoroughly, then cut it off the plywood board. Refer to Painting Removal instructions on page 27. Sign your painting.

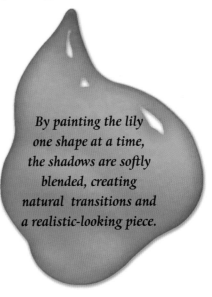

By painting the lily one shape at a time, the shadows are softly blended, creating natural transitions and a realistic-looking piece.

3
Project

Materials:

- Brushes: #1 round, #4 round, 1/2" flat, 1" flat

- Clear water basin

- Craft knife or razor blade

- Disposable brush

- Eraser

- Liquid masking fluid

- Paper towel

- Pencil

- Prepared watercolor palette (Refer to Palette Preparation on pages 14–15)

- Rinse water basin

- Sea sponge

- Spray bottle

- Watercolor paper, 15" x 22"

How do I create a monochromatic painting in warm tones?

Monochromatic basically means "one hue." This will be very similar to the black-and-white painting in the previous project. However, we will use a variety of warm colors instead of just black. Warmth is associated with the colors on the color wheel between yellow and red. This includes brown, orange, and even some redder tones of violet. Cool colors are on the other side of the wheel, and include green, blue, violet, and yellow-green.

1. Tear and stretch your watercolor paper. Refer to Paper Stretching instructions on pages 16–17.

2. Transfer the image onto the paper. Refer to Image Transferring instructions on pages 20–21.

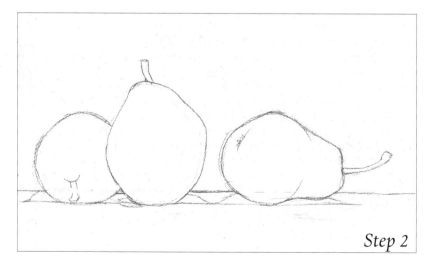

Step 2

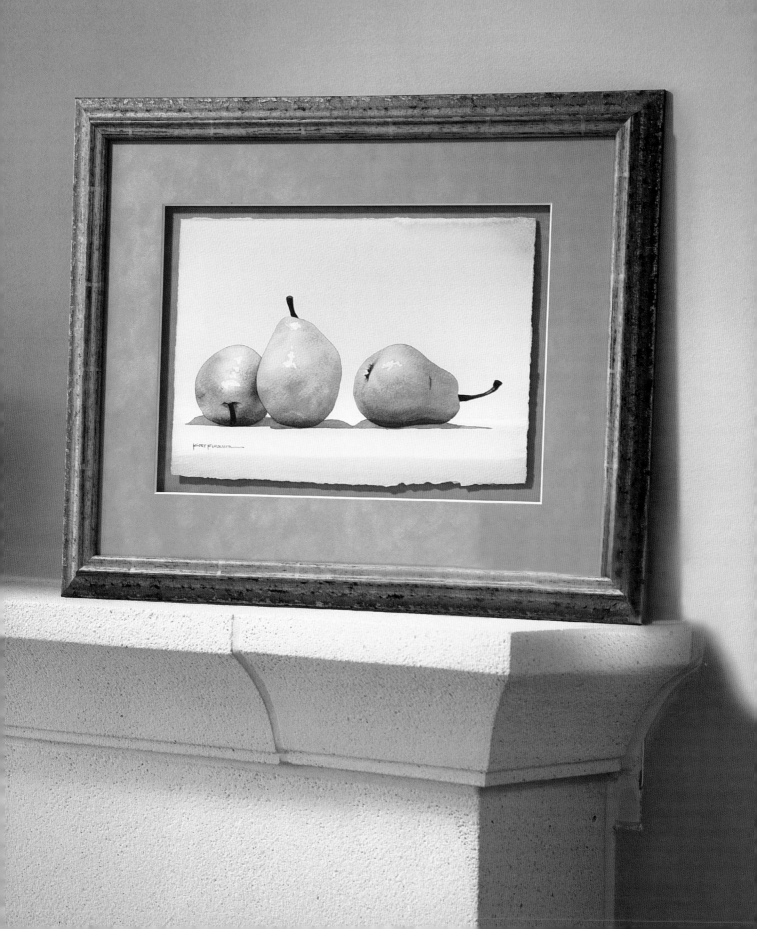

3. Mask the highlights. Refer to Steps 3–4 for Technique Six on pages 50-52.

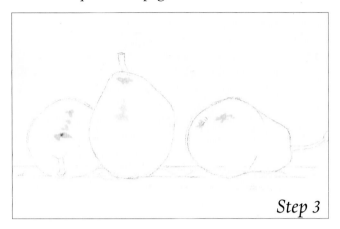

Step 3

4. Using the 1" flat, create a warm wash of Yellow Ochre and Burnt Sienna. Allow the wash to fade, or grow progressively lighter, as you paint downward.

Step 4

5. Still using the 1" flat, wash the base in warm tones that are slightly grayer. Allow to dry thoroughly.

Step 5

6. Paint a wash over the first pear shape, using the #4 round.

7. Switch to the ½" flat, and use the "chasing" technique to create some lighter spots around the highlights. Refer to Step 8 for Technique Four on page 41.

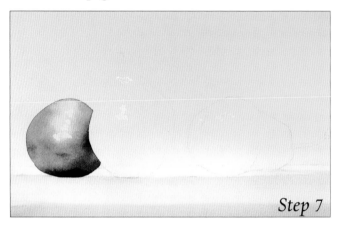

Step 7

8. Skip the adjacent pear and move to the third pear. Create a single wash similar to the first. Do not add any detail yet. Allow to dry thoroughly.

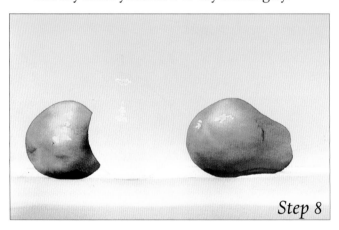

Step 8

9. Paint the middle pear in the same manner as the first two.

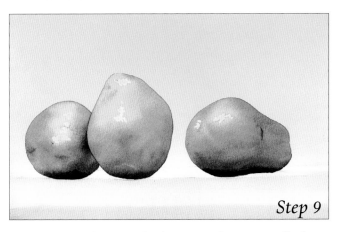

Step 9

10. To paint the cast shadows, apply a controlled wash. Refer to Technique Two on pages 28–33.

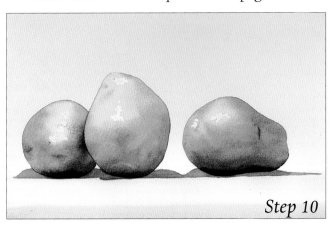

Step 10

11. Lift off the masking fluid to reveal bright white spots. Refer to Steps 12–14 for Technique Six.

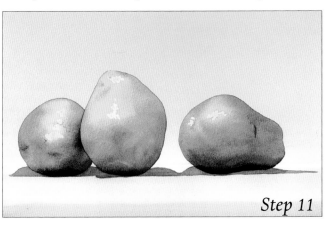

Step 11

12. Using the #4 round, add dark Burnt Umber stems and other details. Switch to the #1 round, and paint clear water around the edge of the highlights to soften the transition.

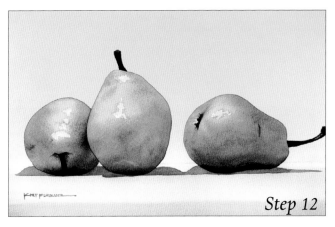

Step 12

13. Allow the painting to dry thoroughly, then cut it off the plywood board. Refer to Painting Removal instructions on page 27. Sign your painting.

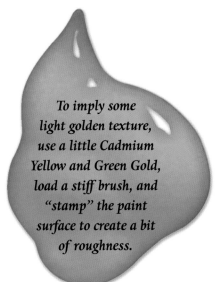

To imply some light golden texture, use a little Cadmium Yellow and Green Gold, load a stiff brush, and "stamp" the paint surface to create a bit of roughness.

4
Project

Materials:

- Brushes: #1 round, #4 round, 1" flat,

- Clear water basin

- Craft knife or razor blade

- Disposable brush

- Eraser

- Liquid masking fluid

- Paper towel

- Pencil

- Prepared watercolor palette (Refer to Palette Preparation on pages 14–15)

- Rinse water basin

- Sea sponge

- Spray bottle

- Watercolor paper, 15" x 22"

How do I create a monochromatic painting in cool tones?

This project will again involve a severely limited palette, this time, using cool tones. *Note: Notice the difference in the overall "feel" of the painting in warm tones vs. the painting in cool tones.*

1. Tear and stretch your watercolor paper. Refer to Paper Stretching instructions on pages 16–17.

2. Transfer the image onto the paper. Refer to Image Transferring instructions on pages 20–21.

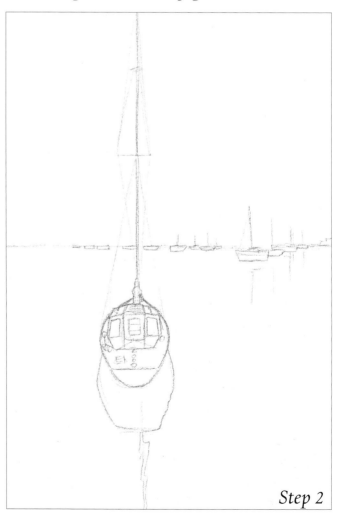

Step 2

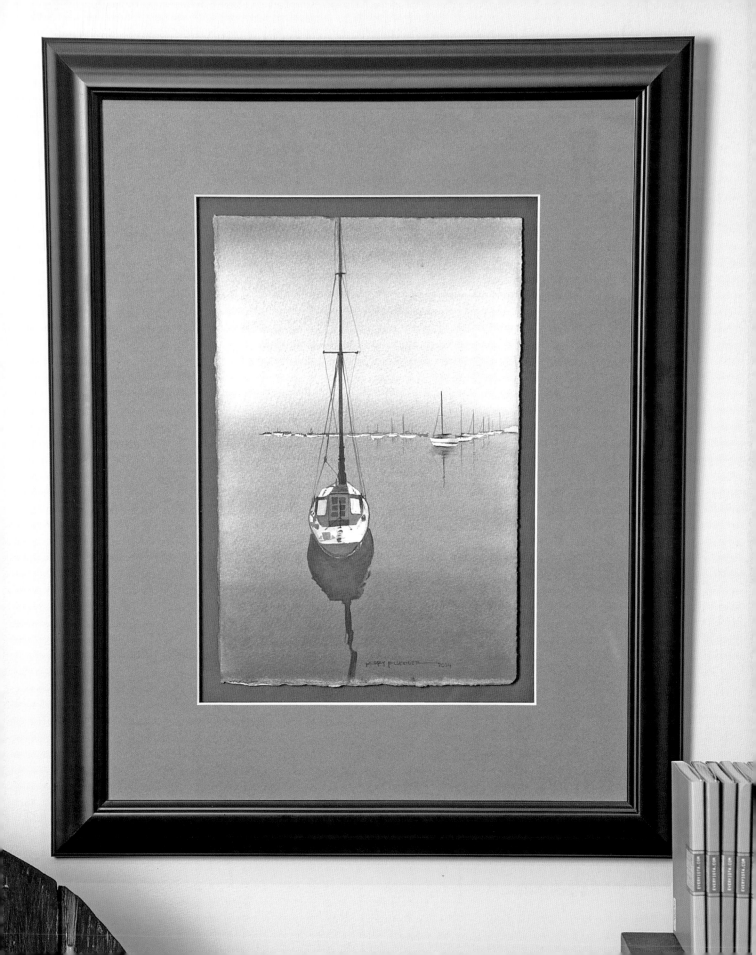

3. Mask off the areas that will remain white. Refer to masking instructions in Steps 3–4 for Technique Six on pages 50–52. *Note: Keep in mind that you only need mask off the areas that are going to be lighter than your background or a completely different color. Since this painting is monochromatic, you only need to think about the value, so only the areas lighter than the background wash need to be masked.*

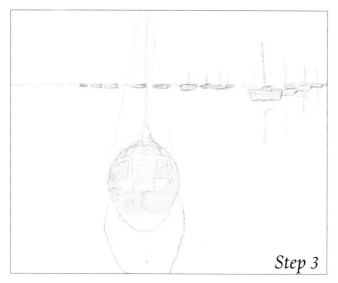

Step 3

4. Using the 1" flat, create a smooth wash with Ultramarine Blue and Ivory Black. Leave a soft transition at the horizon line, implying a light fog. Leave the sky slightly lighter than the area that will be water. Allow to dry.

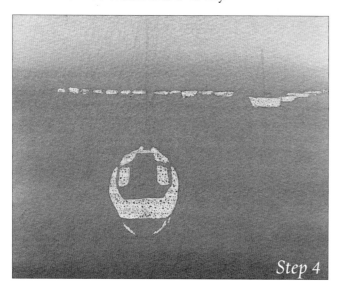

Step 4

5. Remove the masking fluid. Refer to Steps 11–12 for Technique Six.

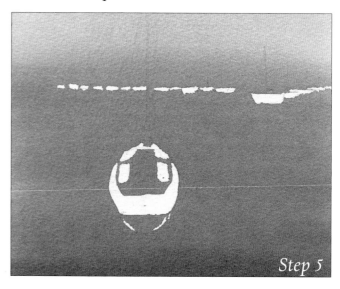

Step 5

6. Use the #1 round to add detail to the distant boats. *Note: Very little detail is required to create the illusion of boats.*

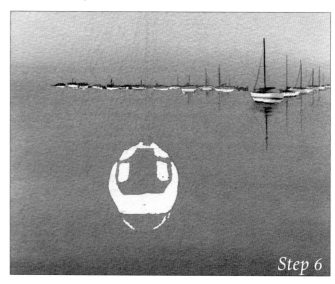

Step 6

7. Alternating between the #1 and #4 rounds, depending on varying degrees of detail, wash the basic shape of the foreground boat's interior. Begin with the lighter shapes.

8. As the lighter washes dry, paint the dark shapes over the tops of the lighter washes with the #1 round.

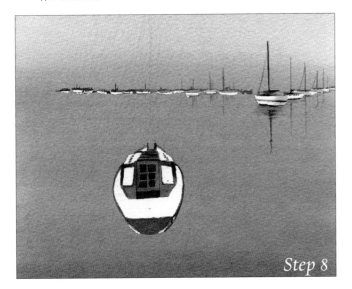

Step 8

9. Using the #4 round, paint the boat's mast and reflection on the water. *Note: Although you want to paint them fairly dark, do not paint them black, as this will overwhelm your painting and draw too much attention away from the focal point.*

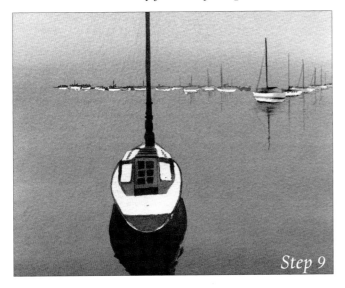

Step 9

10. Add the finishing touches with the #1 round. Wash over some of the deck of the ship with clear water to create the shadow side.

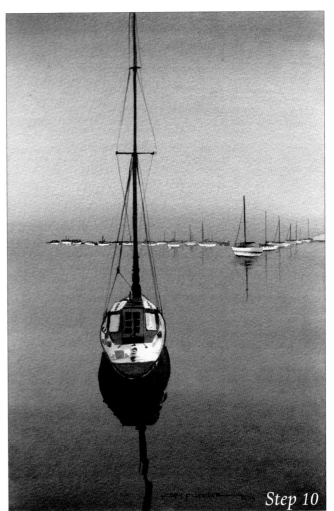

Step 10

11. Allow the painting to dry thoroughly, then cut it off the plywood board. Refer to Painting Removal instructions on page 27. Sign your painting.

Note: Remember, photographs record everything available. In nature, however, your eyes simplify the information they receive. If you imitate a photograph exactly, your painting will look like a photograph. Simplifying your subject as your eyes would in nature will make your painting look more natural, or "real."

5

Project

Materials:

- Brushes: #1 round, #4 round, #10 round, ½" flat, 1" flat

- Clear water basin

- Craft knife or razor blade

- Eraser

- Paper towel

- Pencil

- Prepared watercolor palette (Refer to Palette Preparation on pages 14–15)

- Rinse water basin

- Sea sponge

- Spray bottle

- Watercolor paper, 15" x 22"

How do I create depth in a painting with a wash?

Watercolor is an inherently flat medium. In transparent mediums, building layer upon layer—such as in oil, acrylic, or other opaque mediums—isn't possible. Therefore, creating depth can present a challenge. One way to achieve this effect is to create a blurry wash in the background and sharper detail in the foreground.

1. Tear and stretch your watercolor paper. Refer to Paper Stretching instructions on pages 16–17.

2. Transfer the image onto the paper. Refer to Image Transferring instructions on pages 20–21.

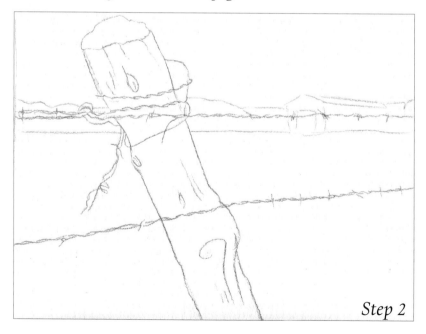

Step 2

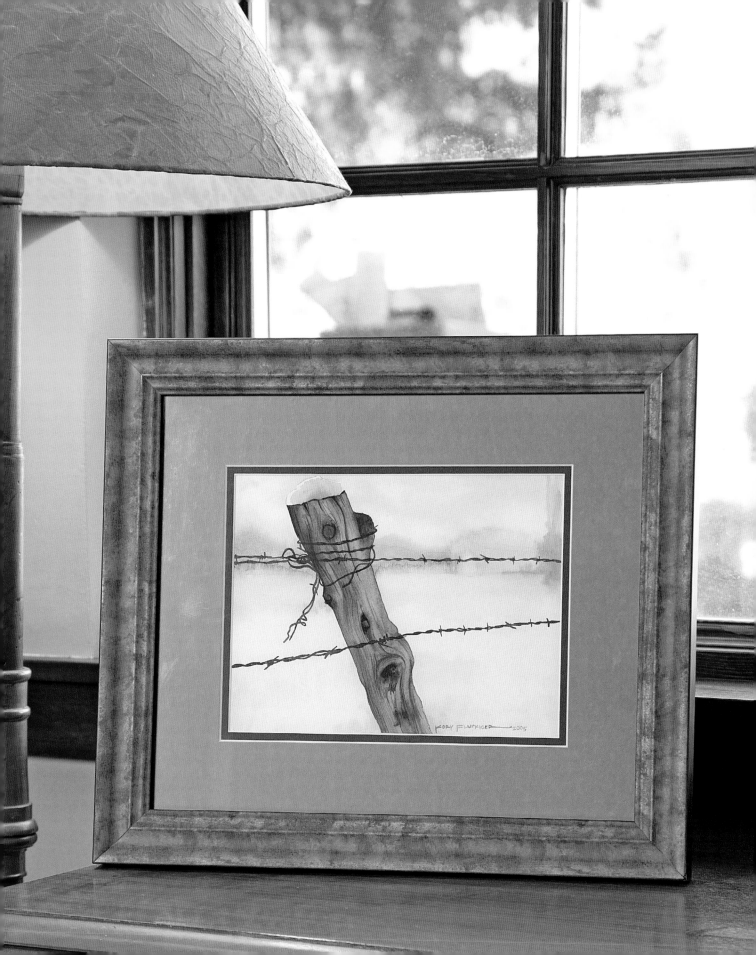

3. Alternating between the ½" flat and 1" flat depending on varying degree of detail, create a wash around the fencepost. Add the detail of the background while the wash is very wet. Allow to dry thoroughly.

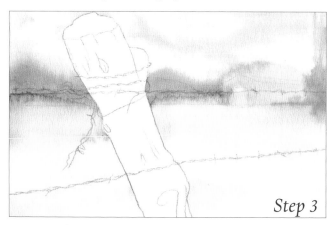
Step 3

4. Using the ½" flat, create a dark wash on the post shape. *Note: Remember, avoid going too dark too quickly. Rather, slowly add colors to build darker values.*

5. While the post is still wet, add in some knots in the wood, allowing them to bleed slightly.

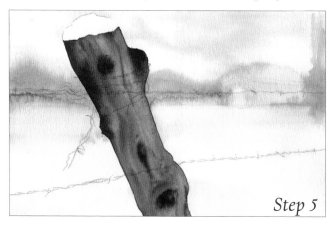
Step 5

6. Alternating between the #4 round, #1 round, and #14 round, depending on varying degree of detail, wash the snow on top of the post with a bit of blue-gray.

7. Use the #1 round to add dark shadows and cracks in the wood. *Note: The wood grain is entirely up to you, so try to have fun creating knots and cracks.*

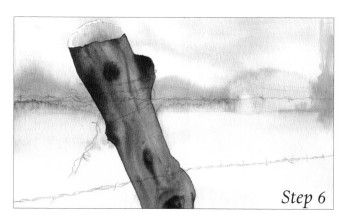
Step 6

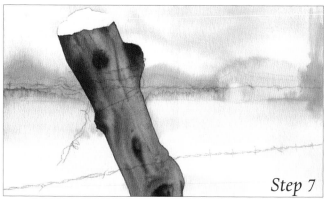
Step 7

8. Allow the wood grain to dry.

9. Using the #1 round, paint the wire as a silhouette. *Note: Make certain the lines of the wire are opaque enough that the wood grain does not show through.*

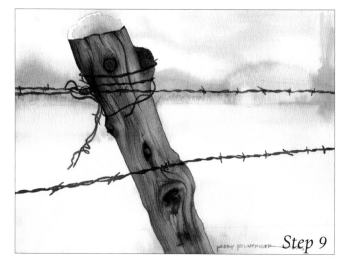
Step 9

10. Allow the painting to dry thoroughly, then cut the paper off the board. Refer to instructions on page 27. Sign your painting.

How do I paint a snowy white landscape with no white paint?

As you may have noticed in the last project, all you have to do to create snow is imply that it is there. The snowy landscape is, more specifically, what you don't paint.

1. Tear and stretch your watercolor paper. Refer to Paper Stretching instructions on pages 16–17.

2. Transfer the image onto the paper. Refer to Image Transferring instructions on pages 20–21.

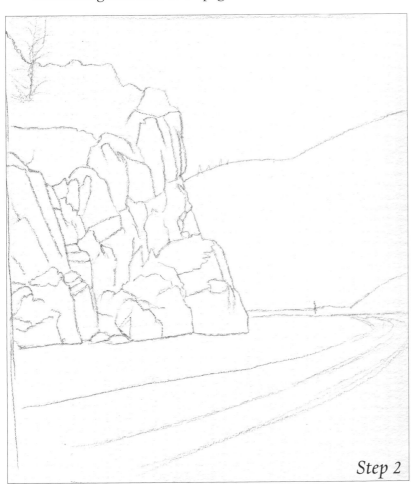

Step 2

6 Project

Materials:

- Brushes: #1 round, #4 round, #10 round, #14 round, ½" flat, 1" flat

- Clear water basin

- Craft knife or razor blade

- Eraser

- Paper towel

- Pencil

- Prepared watercolor palette (Refer to Palette Preparation on pages 14–15)

- Rinse water basin

- Sea sponge

- Spray bottle

- Watercolor paper, 15" x 22"

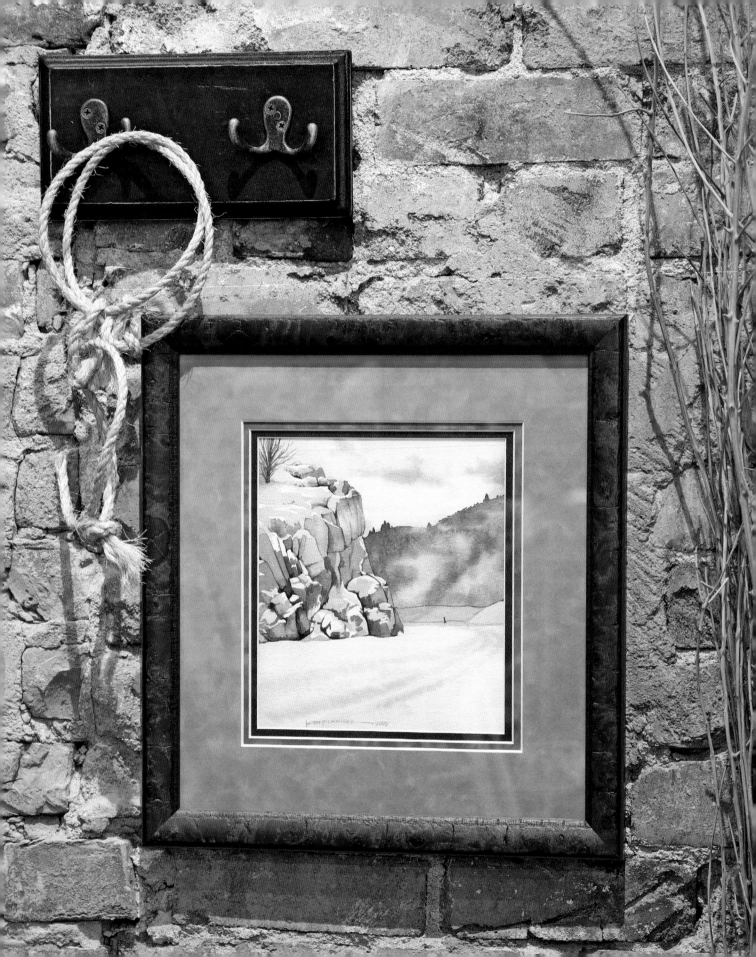

3. Using the 1" flat, wet the sky area with clear water.

4. Using the #14 round, dab in touches of Cerulean Blue mixed with a bit of Cobalt. *Note: A few slight blue spots will be sufficient to imply a cloudy sky.* Touch in a bit of blue-gray to give the clouds shape.

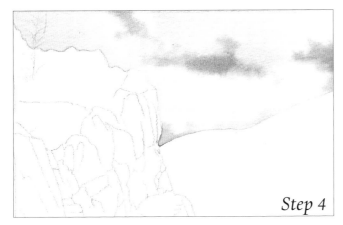

Step 4

5. Using the #10 round, wash the distant mountainside down to the tree line, keeping the overall tone of the wash blue. Switching to the #4 round, touch in some dark spots to imply trees. Touch in some darker spots for trees above the mountain line to create a winter forest skyline.

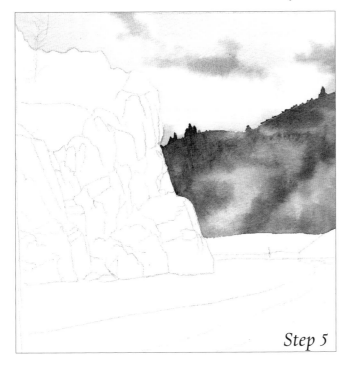

Step 5

6. Alternating between the #10 round and the #4 round, depending on varying degrees of detail, lay in a blue-gray wash from the tree line to the ice line of the reservoir. Allow to dry.

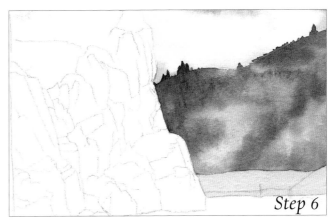

Step 6

7. Add in a bit more blue-gray along the distant mountain ridge.

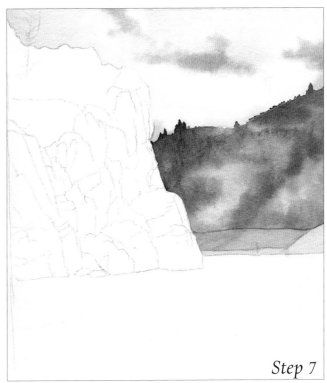

Step 7

8. Define the shape of the icy reservoir with clear water.

9. Touch a bit of blue along the outside edge. Allow the blue to bleed into the wet shape.

10. Paint somewhat of a blue dotted line to emulate snowmobile tracks. Use more blue-gray.

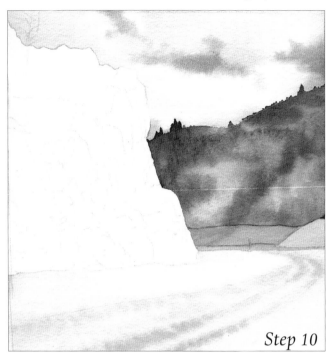

Step 10

11. The cliff is comprised of many individual washes of similar colors. Randomly select which shapes to fill in, skipping the spaces in between for the moment. Allow to dry.

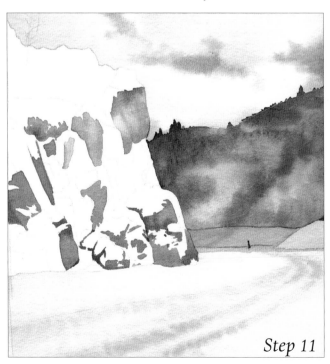

Step 11

12. Continue painting the spaces adjacent to the now-dry washes. *Note: Don't worry too much if you accidentally paint an area intended to be snow. Just treat it as rock.*

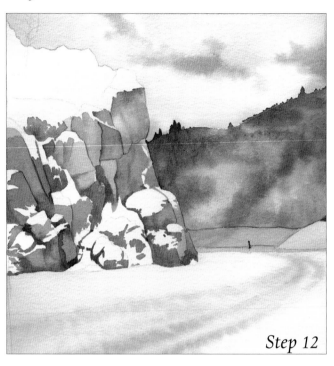

Step 12

13. Once all rocks have their basic washes in place, begin adding some darker edges to help define the rocks. Paint in the small ice fisherman in the distance, remembering to simplify.

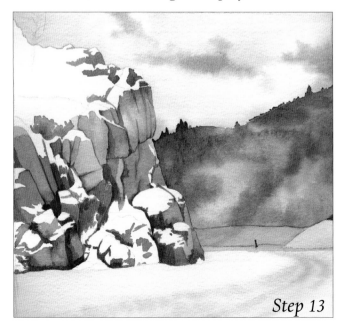

Step 13

14. To paint some blue shadows on the snow, avoid treating it as a wash, but as a detail application as covered in Technique Three on pages 34-37.

15. Paint in some darker edges in the deep shadow spots of the rocks.

16. Place a tree atop the cliff with the #1 round, making fluid strokes upward and outward from the trunk of the tree.

17. Allow the painting to dry thoroughly, then cut it off the plywood board. Refer to Painting Removal instructions on page 27. Sign your painting.

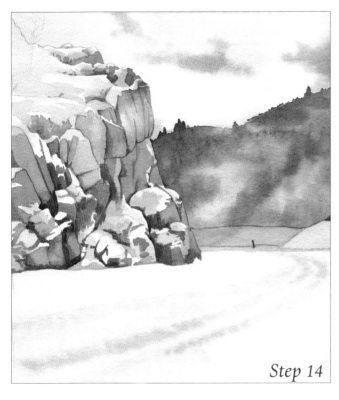

Step 14

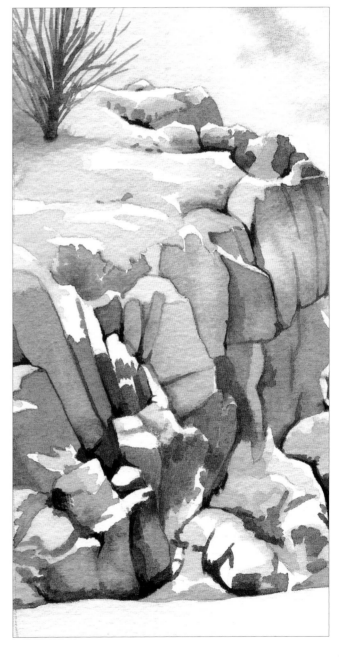

Step 16

7
Project

Materials:

- Brushes: #1 round, #4 round, #10 round, #14 round, ½" flat, 1" flat

- Clear water basin

- Craft knife or razor blade

- Eraser

- Paper towel

- Pencil

- Prepared watercolor palette (Refer to Palette Preparation on pages 14–15)

- Rinse water basin

- Sea sponge

- Spray bottle

- Watercolor paper, 15" x 22"

How do I paint difficult materials such as drapery or glass?

Drapery is sometimes an intimidating subject since the transition between the washes can be subtle. The trick is to break it down into manageable shapes. While painting glass may seem difficult, it's really no different than anything else covered thus far. Remember: Just think of it as simple shapes into which washes are applied.

1. Tear and stretch your watercolor paper. Refer to Paper Stretching instructions on pages 16–17.

2. Transfer the image onto paper. Refer to Image Transferring instructions on pages 20–21.

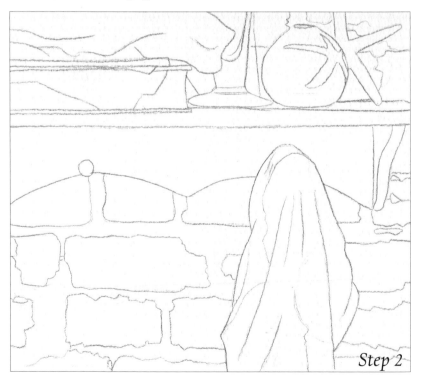

Step 2

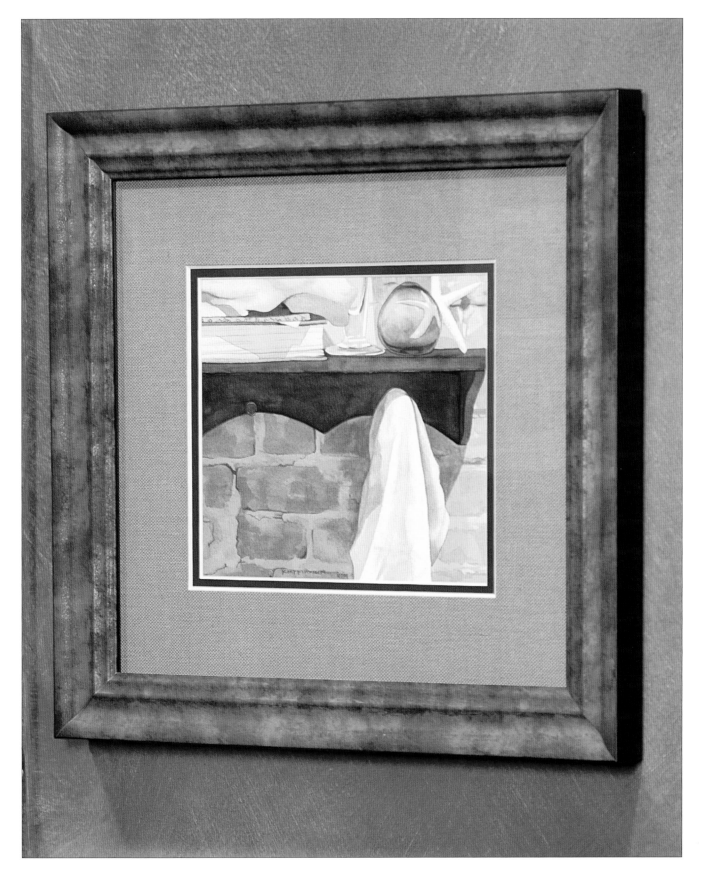

3. Using the 1" flat, lay a light brown wash over the brick background.

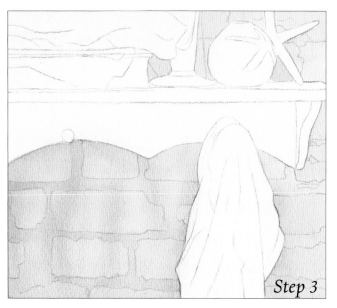

Step 3

4. Switching to the ½" flat, paint a slightly darker wash over each brick.

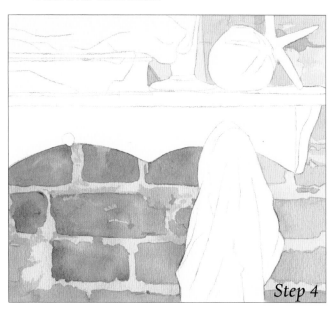

Step 4

5. Using the #14 round, create a wash over some of the bricks for the cast shadows.

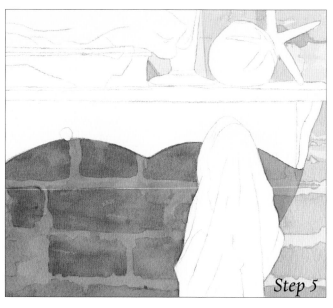

Step 5

6. Using the #4 round, add a few details to define the edges of the bricks.

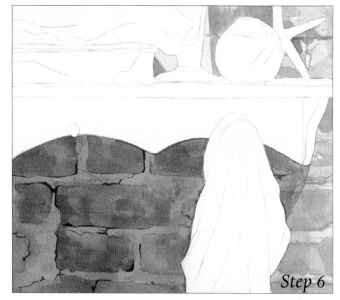

Step 6

7. Continuing with the #4, start the drapery with a wash around the outside folds.

8. Switch to the #10 round. Paint the fold on the right side with the stronger shadow, adding a darker brown along the left edge while it is still slightly wet.

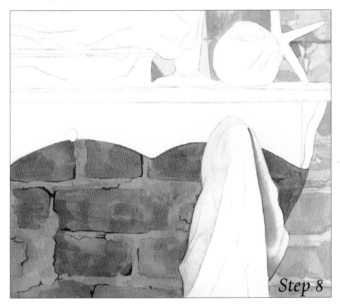

Step 8

9. Continuing with the #10, apply a wash over the center area, allowing the shadow to bleed a bit. This will create the appearance of a soft undulation in the cloth.

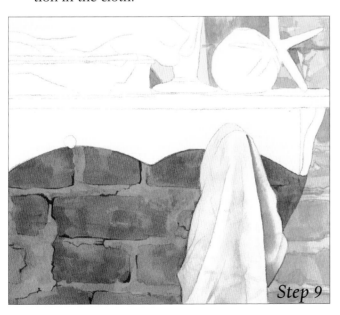

Step 9

10. Using the #4 round, create a darker wash over the left side of the cloth, to create shadows. *Note: Be careful not to muddy highlights or overwork the wash.*

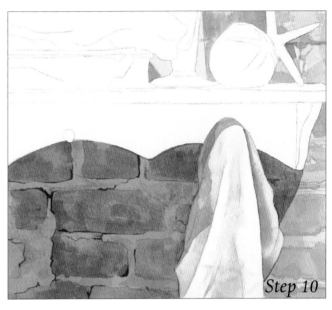

Step 10

11. Using the #14 round, wash the back side of the shelf with a dark brown mixture. Build the dark color up gradually so as not to overpaint one particular spot. Leave the light spot where the left-side hanger is, as it will be lighter than the rest of the shelf back.

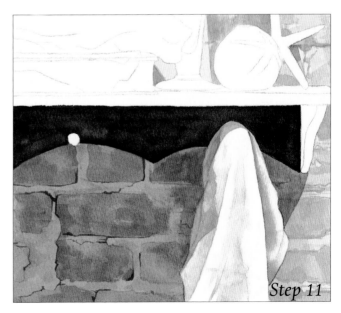

Step 11

12. Alternating between the #4 round and ½" flat, depending on varying degrees of detail, apply a light wash over the left hanger and front edge of the shelf support. Make the top and middle of the support a bit darker to imply the curve of the surface. Allow to dry.

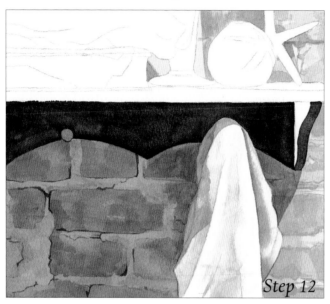

Step 12

13. Using the #4 round, paint the dark side of the support and the top of the shelf. Paint a darker circle inside the light hanger, leaving a light ring around the edge where the wood is worn.

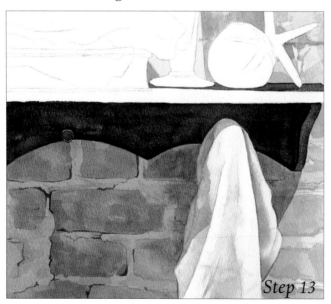

Step 13

14. Alternating between the #10 round and ½" flat, depending on varying degrees of detail, wash the front edge of the shelf. Drop in some subtle variations and soft shadows for added interest.

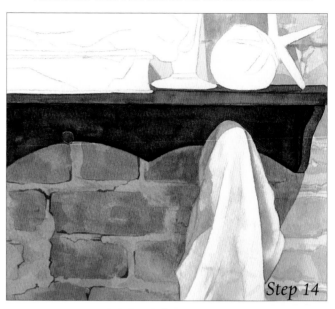

Step 14

15. Using the ½" flat, paint the glass ball by creating a wash around the distorted sea star. Switch to the #4 round to paint in the darker edges. Leave the middle fairly light to create the round appearance. With the #1 round, very lightly paint a few spots on the sea star to add texture.

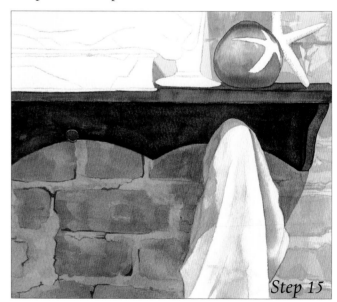

Step 15

16. Using the #4 round, add a light wash over the distorted sea star image to create shape. Wash the shadows in the clear vase.

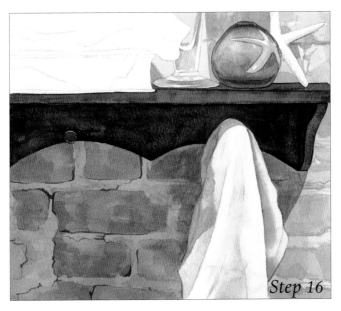

Step 16

17. With the #14 round, lay a light wash over the rag, similar to that used on the hanging cloth. Create some soft shadows. Begin to block in the books with light, simple washes.

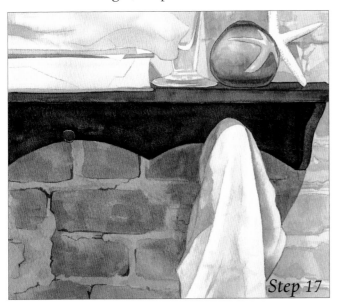

Step 17

18. Paint shadows on the cloth and book pages with the #4 round.

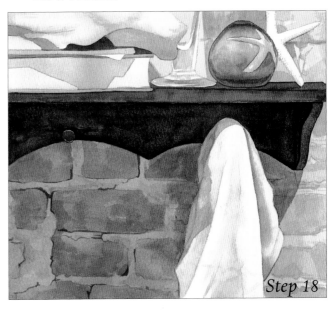

Step 18

19. Use the #1 round to add all of the fine detail work. Darken the deep shadows, then create the book's pages and decorative binding.

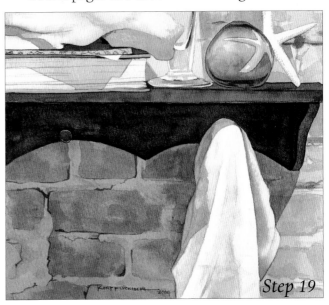

Step 19

20. Allow the painting to dry thoroughly, then cut it off the plywood board. Refer to Painting Removal instructions on page 27. Sign your painting.

8
Project

Materials:

- Brushes: #1 round, #4 round, $\frac{1}{2}$" flat, 1" flat

- Clear water basin

- Craft knife or razor blade

- Eraser

- Paper towel

- Pencil

- Prepared watercolor palette (Refer to Palette Preparation on pages 14–15)

- Rinse water basin

- Sea sponge

- Spray bottle

- Watercolor paper, (3) sheets of 15" x 22"

How do I create a vertical triptych with an oriental look?

This piece will be a triptych, or a series of three paintings, which together make a whole. Although this project incorporates three pieces of the same image, a triptych doesn't necessarily have to be so. It simply means that the paintings belong together.

This project is quick and easy to create, yet maintains a classic look. We will create a vertical triptych, which will hang on the wall like a scroll.

1. Tear and stretch the sheets of paper. Refer to Paper Stretching instructions on pages 16–17.

2. Transfer the image onto the paper. Refer to Image Transferring instructions on pages 20–21.

3. Begin with the large bamboo stalk. Alternating between the $\frac{1}{2}$" and 1" flats, depending on the width of the subject, paint a separate wash for each section of the bamboo stalks. To keep the painting consistent, work on all three panels simultaneously.

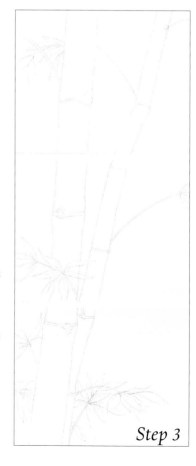

Step 3

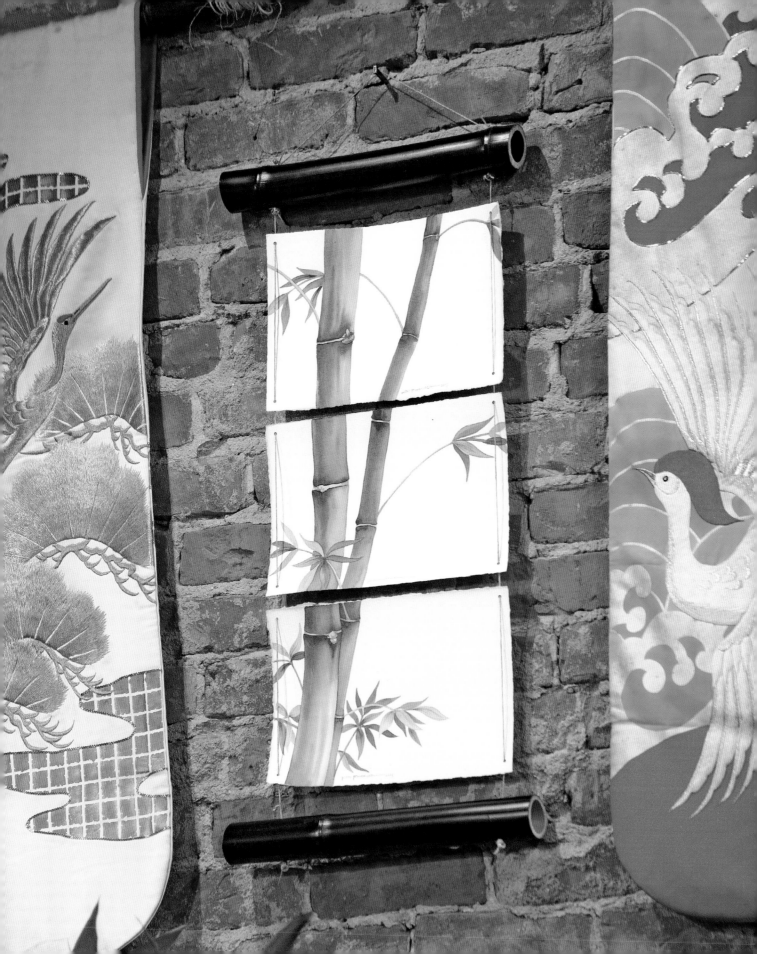

4. Using the ¹/₂" flat, touch the paint in near the bamboo joints to keep the color very rich. Pull the green through the rest of the stem by stroking the paint in vertical motions.

5. Paint the small stalk in the same manner, alternating between the ¹/₂" and 1" flats.

6. Using the #14 round, color in the branches and leaves with simple controlled washes. Refer to Technique Two on pages 28–33. Allow to dry.

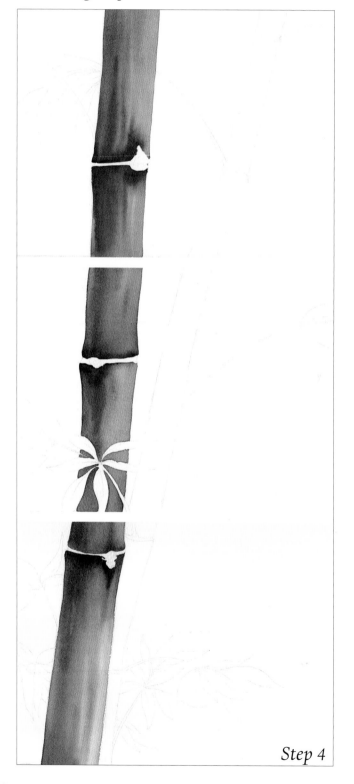

Step 4

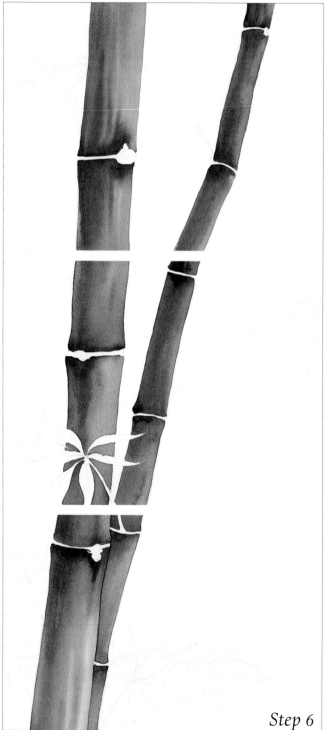

Step 6

7. Fill in the other leaves and branches.

8. Use the #1 round to fill in the joints of the bamboo and add detail to the leaves.

9. Allow the painting to dry thoroughly, then cut it off the plywood board. Refer to Painting Removal instructions on page 27. Sign your painting.

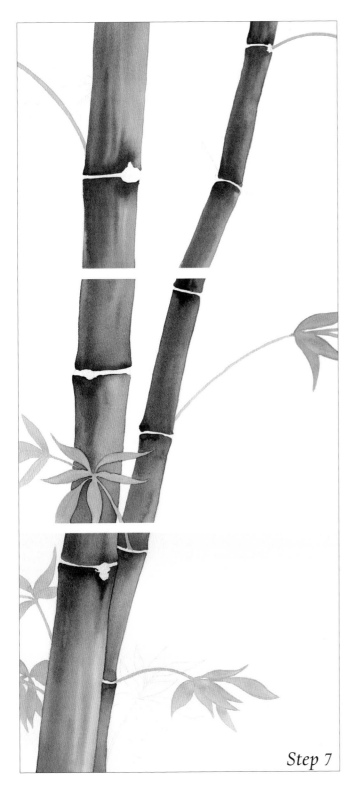

Step 7

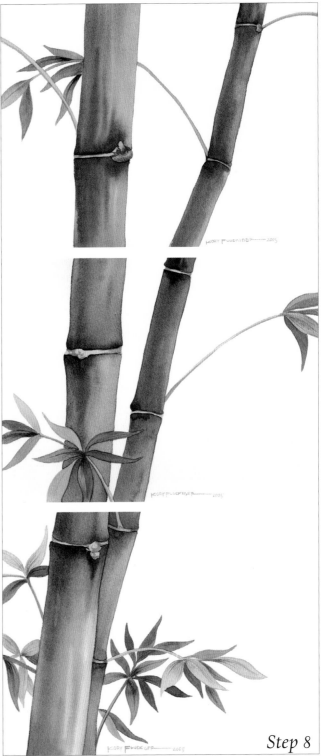

Step 8

9
Project

Materials:

- Brushes: #1 round, #4 round, 1" flat

- Clear water basin

- Craft knife or razor blade

- Disposable brush

- Eraser

- Liquid masking fluid

- Paper towel

- Pencil

- Prepared watercolor palette (Refer to Palette Preparation on pages 14–15)

- Rinse water basin

- Sea sponge

- Spray bottle

- Toothbrush

- Watercolor paper, 8$\frac{1}{2}$" x 11"

How do I paint for stationery?

Watercolor is an effective medium for creating stationery. The trick to creating stationery is to paint accent decorations and leave most of the page clear for writing.

1. Tear and stretch your watercolor paper. Refer to Paper Stretching instructions on pages 16–17. *Note: The size is not as important as the proportions, because the paper can be sized during color copying.*

2. Transfer the image onto the paper. Refer to Image Transferring instructions on pages 20–21.

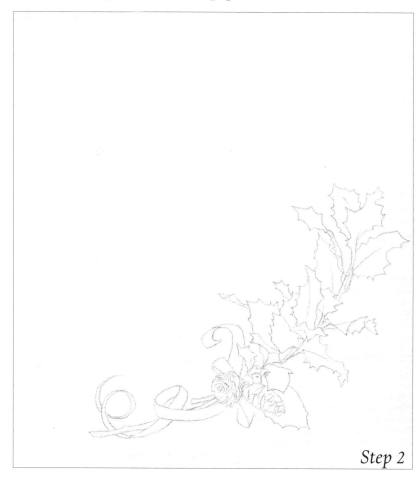

Step 2

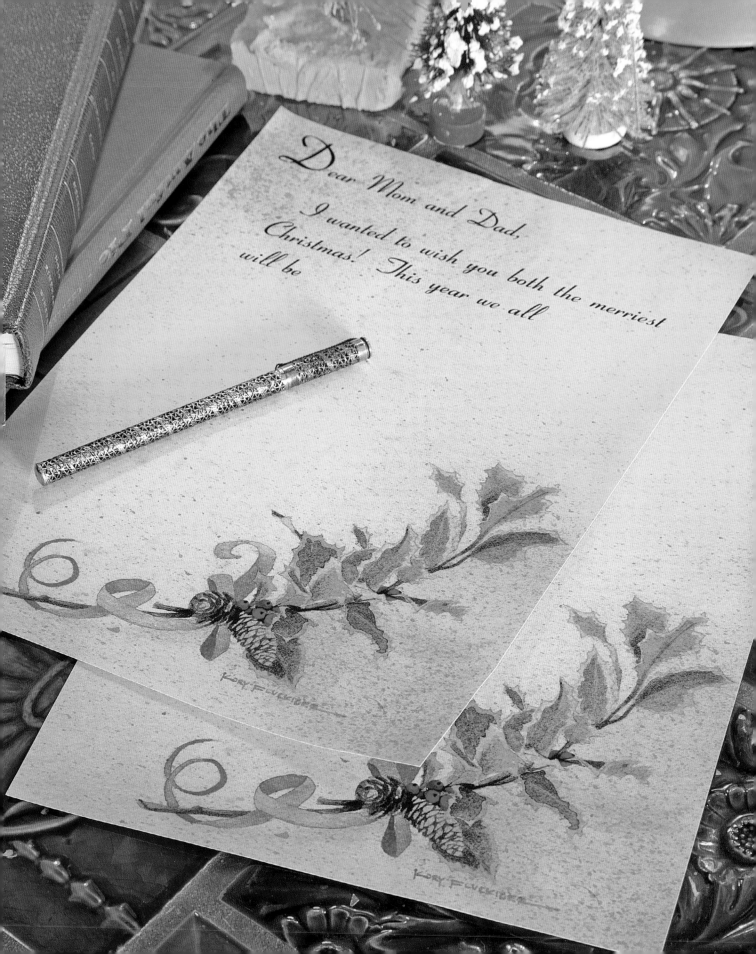

Dear Mom and Dad,

I wanted to wish you both the merriest Christmas! This year we all will be

3. Using the 1" flat, apply an overall wash with some light browns and yellows. Lightly spatter while the wash is still wet. Refer to Steps 15–17 in Technique Five on pages 44–49. Paint a light, soft shadow near the subject, using the 1" flat. Allow to dry.

Step 3

4. Repeat spattering.

Step 4

Step 5

5. Using the #4 round, lightly paint the red ribbon with a simple controlled wash. Refer to Technique Two on pages 28–33. Allow to dry.

6. Add the shaded sides of the ribbon.

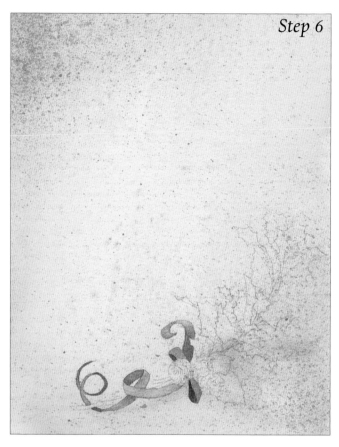

Step 6

7. Wash the pinecones with a light Yellow Ochre.

8. Paint the details on the pinecones with dark Van Dyke Brown.

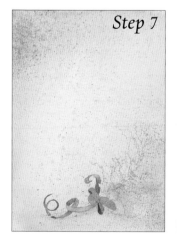

Step 7

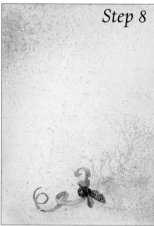

Step 8

9. Apply a simple controlled wash over the holly stems and leaves with a mixture of Green Gold and Hooker's Green.

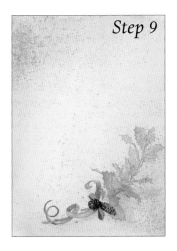

Step 9

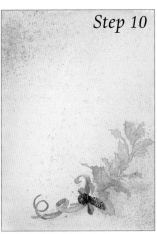

Step 10

10. Add detail with a bit more Hooker's Green. *Note: Be certain to leave the edge lighter, as this is what will create the variegated effect.*

11. Paint the berries with a bright Cadmium Red.

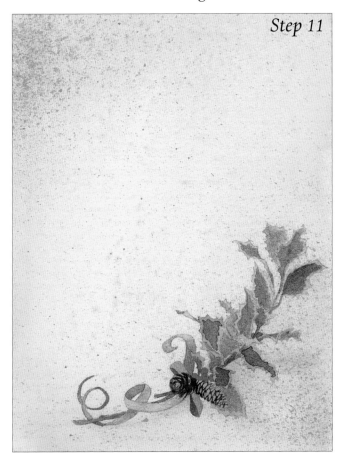

Step 11

12. Switching back to the #1 round touch in the darker shadows and final details.

Step 12

13. Allow the painting to dry thoroughly, then cut it off the plywood board. Refer to Painting Removal instructions on page 27. Sign your painting.

Note: I recommend taking the painting to the copy store to produce multiple color copies. This way, you can use the design again.

10 Project

Materials:

- Brushes: #1 round, #4 round, 1" flat
- Clear water basin
- Craft knife or razor blade
- Eraser
- Paper towel
- Pencil
- Prepared watercolor palette (Refer to Palette Preparation on pages 14–15)
- Rinse water basin
- Sea sponge
- Spray bottle
- Toothbrush
- Watercolor paper, 2" x 8½"

How do I paint a bookmark?

Hand-painted bookmarks can make great gifts, or something to use for yourself. To paint a bookmark that matches your stationery, follow the instructions in Project 9 on pages 90–93. Simply change the design slightly.

1. Tear the paper. Refer to Tearing instructions on pages 16–17. *Note: It is not necessary to stretch the paper for this project, as it is very small.*

2. Transfer the image onto the paper. Refer to Image Transferring instructions on pages 20–21.

3. Using the 1" flat, apply an overall wash with some light browns and yellows. Refer to Technique One on pages 24–27. Allow to dry.

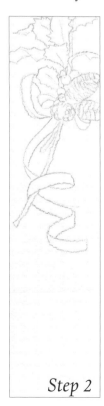
Step 2

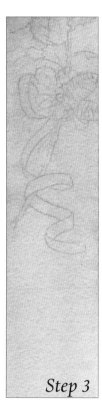
Step 3

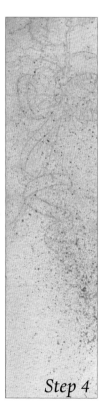
Step 4

DECEMBER

...d house, a naked moor,
...ing pool before the door,
...n bare of flowers or fruit
...ars at the garden foot.
...e place that I live in,
...thout and bare within.

...ur ragged moor pa...
...parable pomp...
...ld glories o...
...ur shivering...
...e wind from p...
...moored cloud...
...en gloom and...
...g sun, with gla...
...the wizard moo...
...s, in the crimson...
...clining splendou...
... of the stars a...
...ouring hollows dry...
...all with tender f...
...e morning muses...
...g from the broom...
...airy wheel and th...
...o dew - bediamond...
...s go, shall winter t...
...simple grass with...
...ost enchant the p...
...the cart-ruts beau...
...now - bright the moor...
...ur children clap the...
...s Earth our hermit...
...and a changeful ph...
...; and intricate devi...
...d seasons doth suff...

R.Z.S.

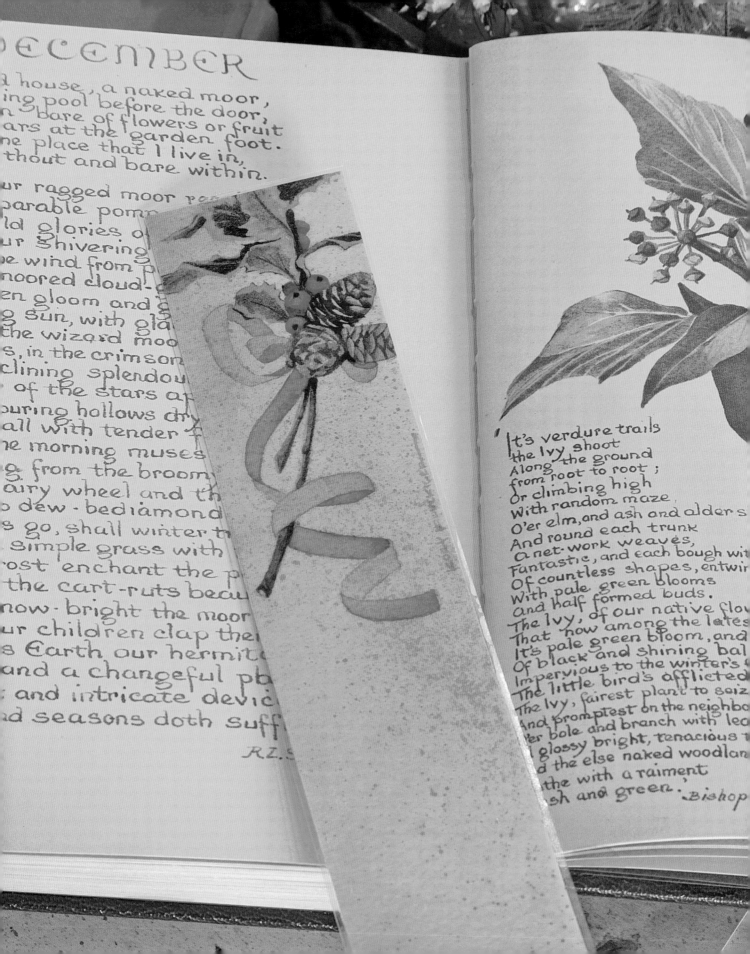

...It's verdure trails
the Ivy shoot
Along the ground
from root to root;
Or climbing high
With random maze,
O'er elm, and ash and alders ...
And round each trunk
A net-work weaves,
Fantastic, and each bough wit...
Of countless shapes, entwi...
With pale green blooms
And half formed buds.
The Ivy, of our native flo...
That 'now among the late...
It's pale green bloom, and...
Of black and shining bal...
Impervious to the winter's...
The little bird's afflicted...
The Ivy, fairest plant to seiz...
And promptest on the neighbo...
...er bole and branch with lea...
...glossy bright, tenacious...
...d the else naked woodlan...
...the with a raiment
...sh and green. Bishop

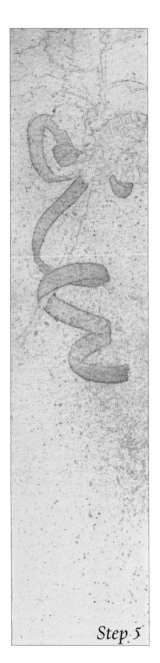

Step 5

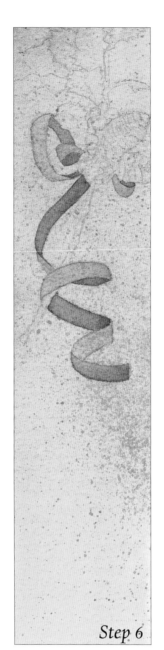

Step 6

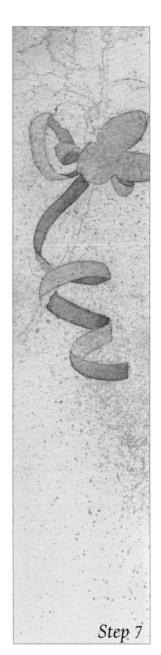

Step 7

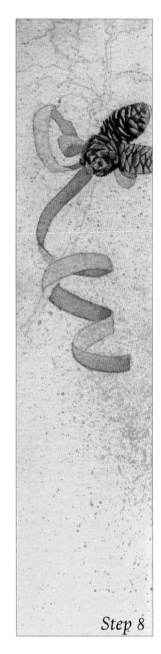

Step 8

4. Spatter the bookmark as explained in Steps 15–17 for Technique Five on page 49.

5. Using the #4 round, paint the red ribbon lightly with a simple controlled wash. Refer to Technique Two on pages 28–33. Allow to dry.

6. Begin to add the shaded sides of the ribbon.

7. Wash the pinecones with a light yellow.

8. Paint the details on the pinecones with dark brown.

9. Apply a simple controlled wash over the holly stems and leaves. *Note: I used a mixture of Green Gold and Hooker's Green.*

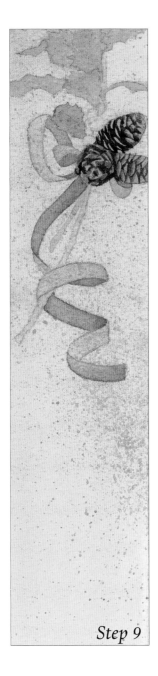

Step 9

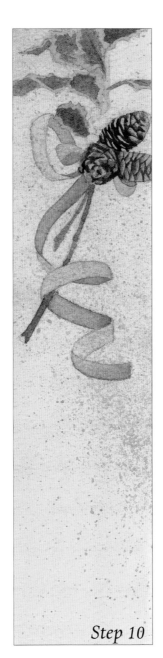

Step 10

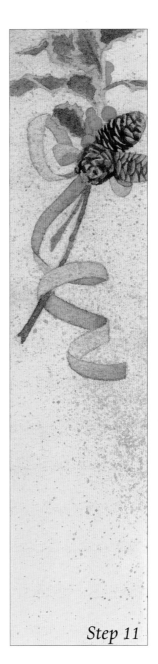

Step 11

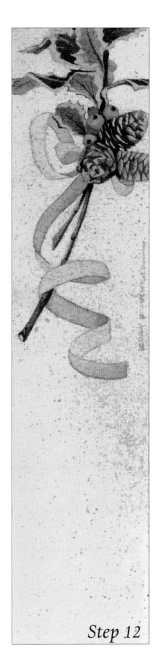

Step 12

10. Add detail with a bit more green. Be certain to leave the edge lighter as this is what will create the variegated effect.

11. Paint the berries with a bright red.

12. Using the #1 round, dab in the darker shadows and final details.

13. Allow the bookmark to dry thoroughly. Sign your painting.

Note: I recommend taking your bookmark to the copy store. Make several copies and have the bookmarks laminated. If you plan to make more copies of your bookmark in the future, avoid using the original painting to mark your book, as it may become damaged from use.

11 Project

Materials:

- Brushes: #1 round, #4 round, #10 round, #14 round, 1" flat

- Clear water basin

- Craft knife or razor blade

- Disposable brush

- Eraser

- Liquid masking fluid

- Paper towel

- Pencil

- Prepared watercolor palette (Refer to Palette Preparation on pages 14–15)

- Rinse water basin

- Sea sponge

- Spray bottle

- Watercolor paper, 12" square

How do I paint for a scrapbook page?

This project will involve painting a silver frame for a scrapbook page. This can add a nice, personal touch to the accent decorations in any scrapbook. As with the stationery and bookmark, the frame painting can be easily reproduced for multiple uses.

1. Tear and stretch your watercolor paper. Refer to Paper Stretching instructions on pages 16–17. *Note: Any size paper will work, although scrapbook pages are traditionally 12" square.*

2. Transfer the image onto the paper. Refer to Image Transferring instructions on pages 20–21. *Note: Do not worry too much about dimension, as photos can be cut to fit inside the frame.*

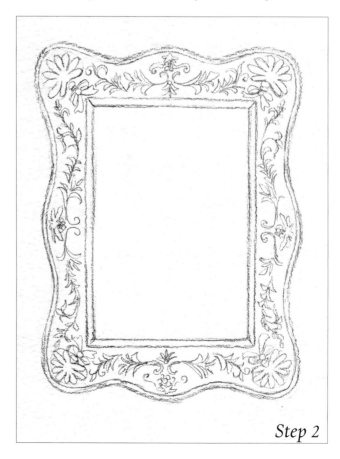

Step 2

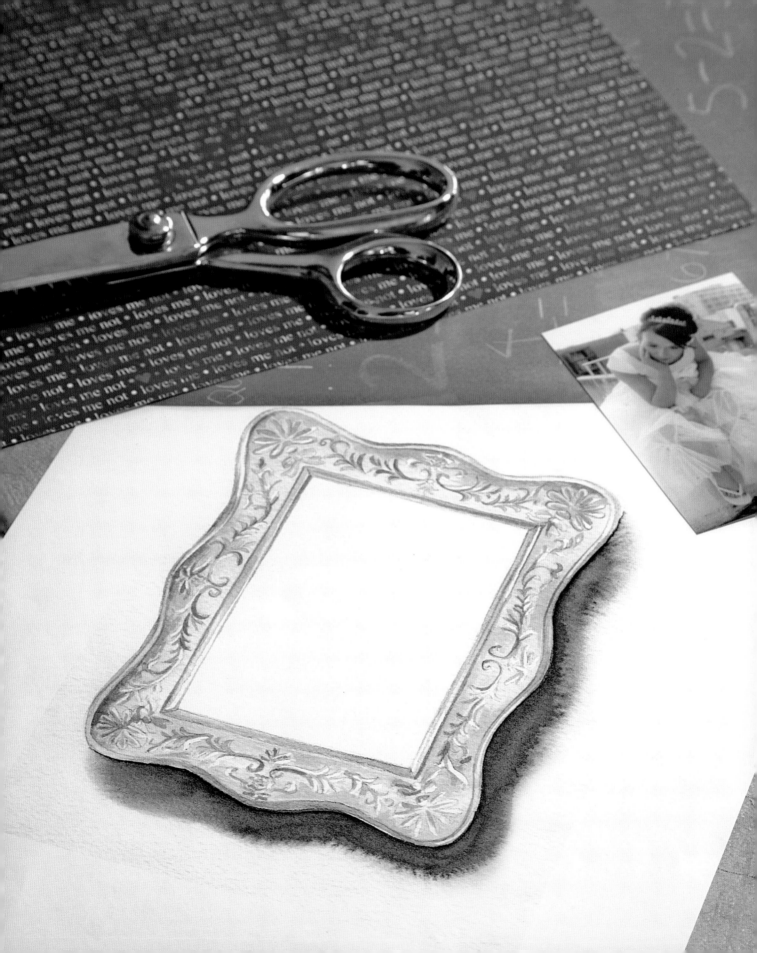

3. Use the masking fluid to create highlights where desired in the frame design. Refer to Steps 3–4 for Technique Six on page 50–52.

4. Alternating between the #4 and #14 rounds, depending on varying degrees of detail, apply a light blue-gray wash over the frame area, leaving some lighter spots to create a metallic effect.

5. Remove the masking fluid to expose the highlights. Refer to Steps 12–14 on page 55.

6. Using the #4 round, touch in some detail, using a slightly darker blue-gray color. Allow some highlights to remain visible.

7. Using the #1 round, paint some scattered deep shadows in darker blue-gray. *Note: Be careful to not exaggerate highlights and shadows, as this can result in an unrealistically contoured, cartoon-like painting.*

8. Using the 1" flat, wash the shadow area with clear water. Spread the water much further than you intend to paint the shadow. Using the #10 round, paint in a soft cast shadow. *Note: The water will allow the shadow to bleed out, creating a smooth transition.*

9. Allow the painting to dry thoroughly, then cut it off the plywood board. Refer to Painting Removal instructions on page 27. Sign your painting.

Note: Use the original or color copies for creating scrapbook pages.

Step 3

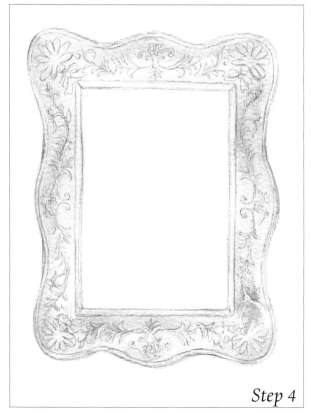

Step 4

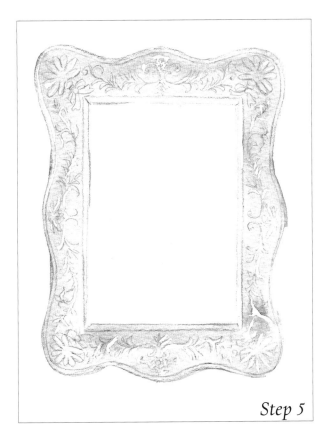

Step 5

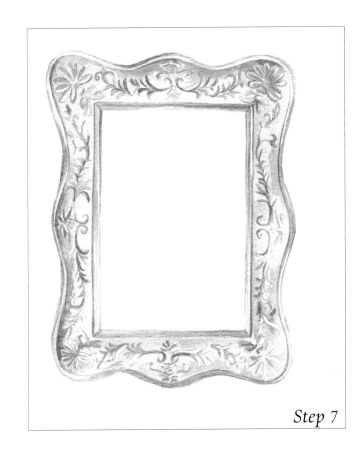

Step 7

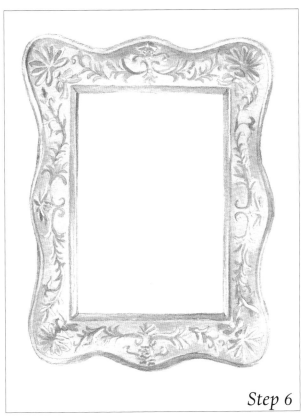

Step 6

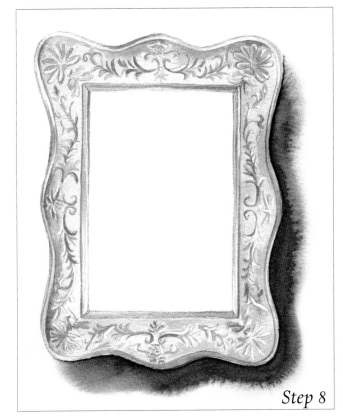

Step 8

12 Project

How do I paint a greeting card?

The stone cupid in this project can be used as the front of a blank note card. Sometimes it's best to let the subject matter speak for itself, rather than complicating the card with words.

Materials:

- Brushes: #1 round, #4 round, #10

- Clear water basin

- Craft knife or razor blade

- Eraser

- Paper towel

- Pencil

- Prepared watercolor palette (Refer to Palette Preparation on pages 14–15)

- Rinse water basin

- Sea sponge

- Spray bottle

- Watercolor paper, 7" x 10"

1. Tear and stretch your watercolor paper. Refer to Paper Stretching instructions on pages 16–17.

2. Transfer the image onto the front of the card. Refer to Image Transferring instructions on pages 20–21.

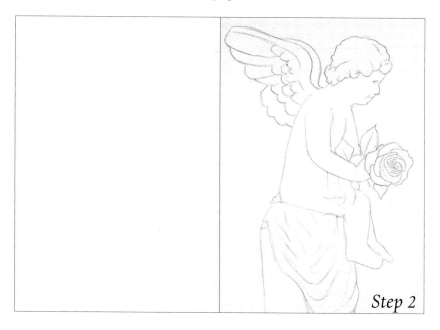

Step 2

Note: Transfer the image onto the right-hand side of the paper, so that once folded, the picture will be on the front of the card.

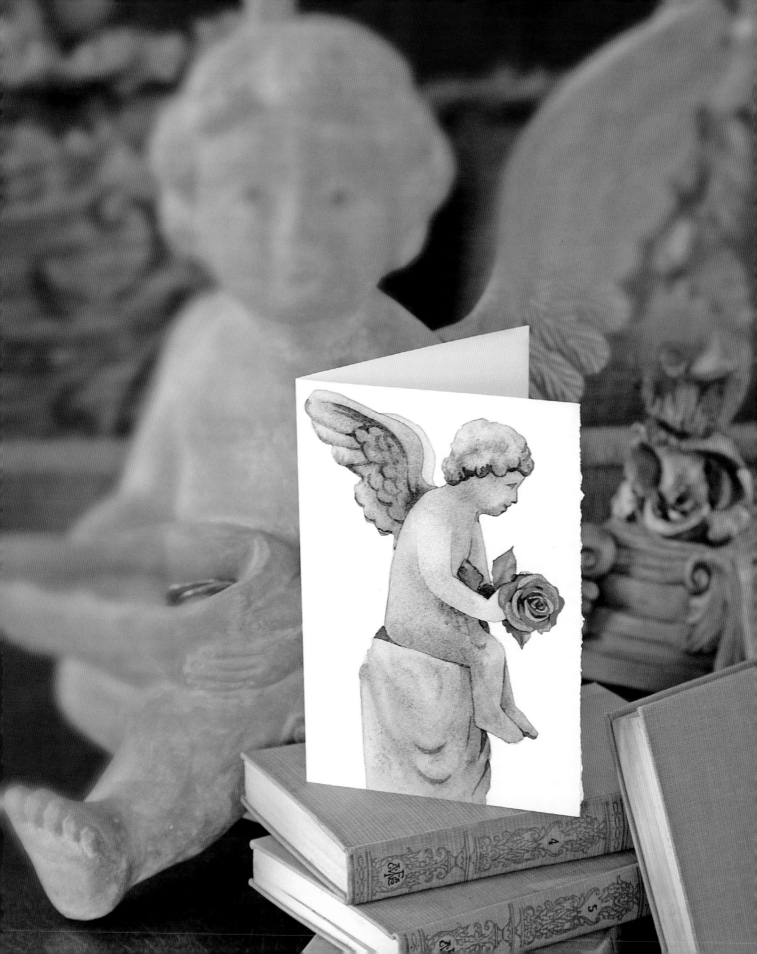

3. Using the #4 round, apply a light red wash over the rose.

4. Alternating between the #4 and #1 rounds, depending on varying degrees of detail, fill in the shadowed areas of the rose bloom with a darker red. *Note: I used a mixture of Cadmium Red and Alizarin Crimson.*

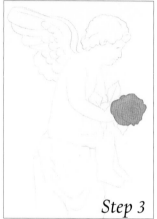

Step 3

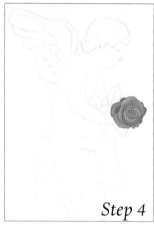

Step 4

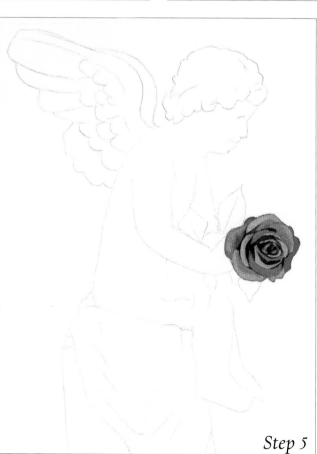

Step 5

5. Using the #1 round, add deeper shadows in the rose with a darker mixture of the same colors. *Note: To avoid graying, try adding a touch of Ultramarine Blue.*

6. Using the #4 round, wash the stem and leaves in green with a controlled wash. Refer to Technique Two on pages 28–33. Add darker shadows while the leaf wash is still wet. Allow to dry.

7. Alternating between the #10 and #4 rounds, depending on varying degrees of detail, create a controlled blue-gray wash over the entire cupid statue. Begin defining basic shadow areas, but do not worry about detail yet. Allow the wash to dry.

8. Using the #4, lay a second wash over the hair for definition. Add shadows to imply the curls.

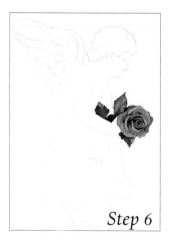

Step 6

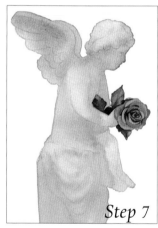

Step 7

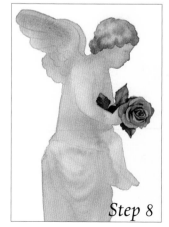

Step 8

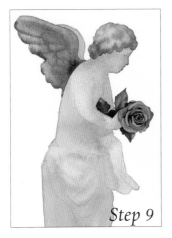

Step 9

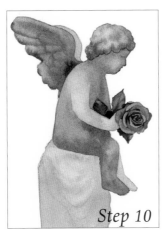

Step 10

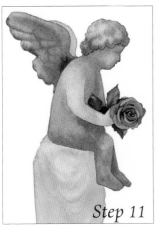

Step 11

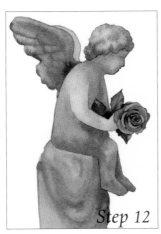

Step 12

13. Switching to the #1 round, add the deep shadows and final details.

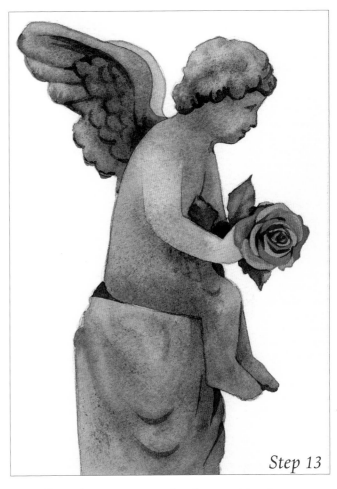

Step 13

9. Continuing with the #4 round, paint in the detail for the forewing in the same manner as the hair.

10. Touch in the detail on the head, body, and foreleg, using a controlled wash of the same blue-gray color. Add some greens and browns for interest. Allow to dry.

11. Paint the other leg separately, using the same technique, as this will allow them to remain visually independent parts of the statue.

12. Alternating between the #4 and the #10 rounds, depending on varying degrees of detail, wash the pedestal to create soft shadows. Touch in more green and brown for added interest, but avoid adding too much or the effect will be overwhelming and the statue will appear somewhat green.

14. Allow the painting to dry thoroughly, then cut the paper off the board. Refer to Painting Removal instructions on page 27.

15. Score and fold the card so that it will measure 5" x 7". *Notes: This size card will fit easily into readymade envelopes. Sign your painting.*

This project makes a festive Valentine's Day card.

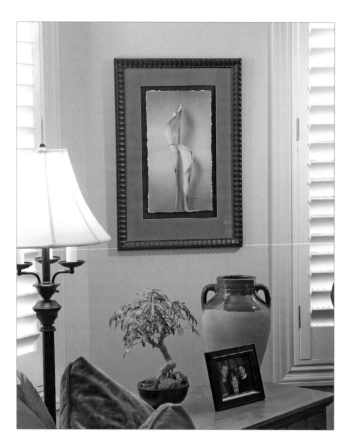

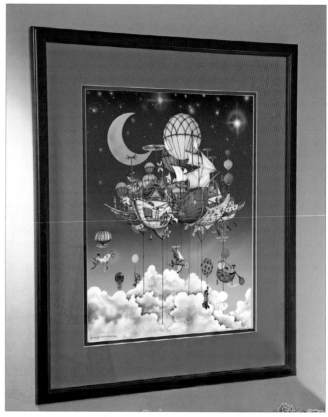

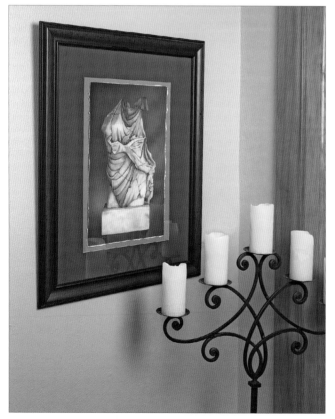

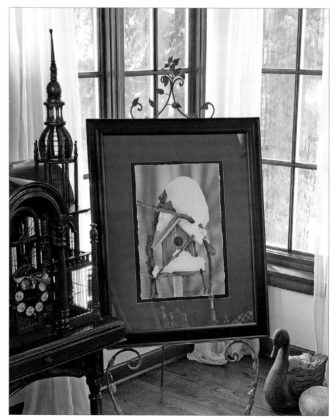

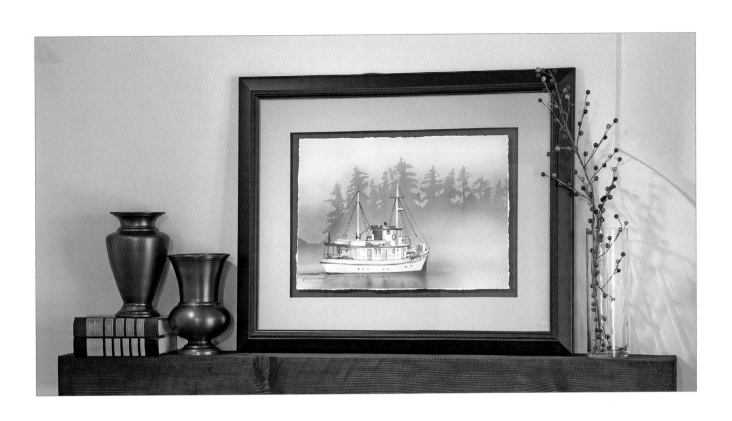

Section 4: *Gallery*

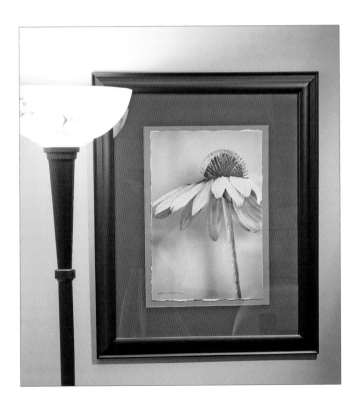

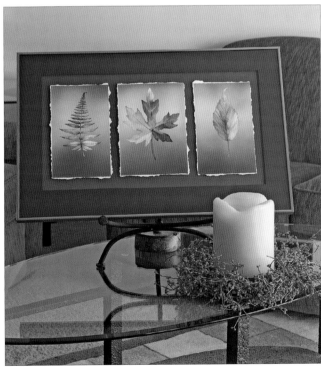

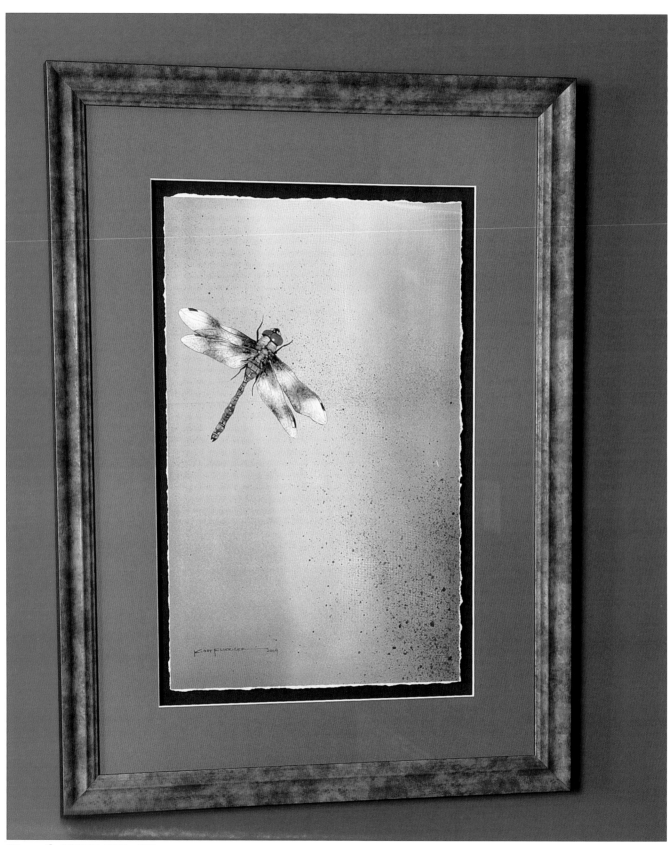

"Dragonfly II" 2004, 10½" x 20"

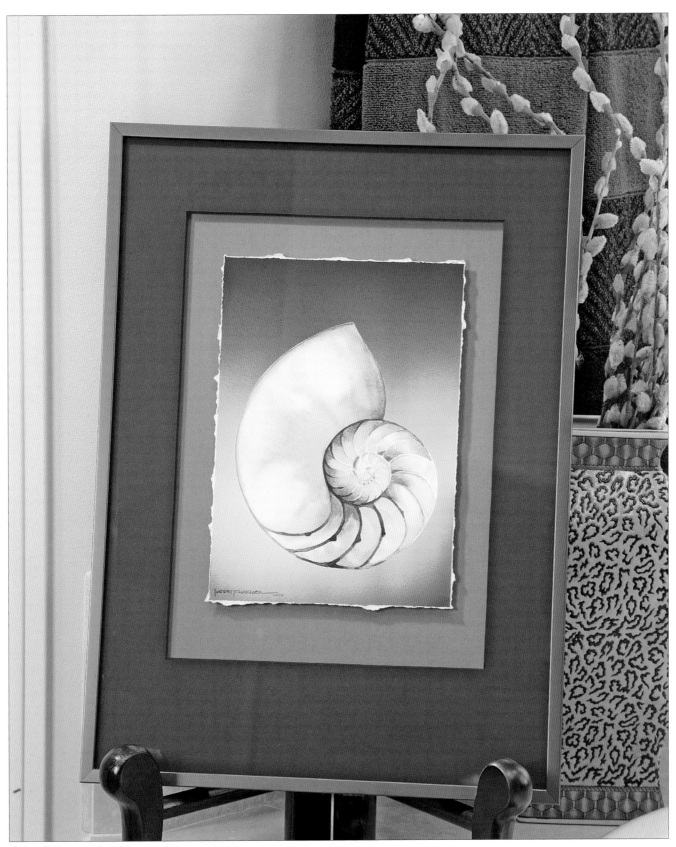

"Nautalis" 2001, 8" x 11"

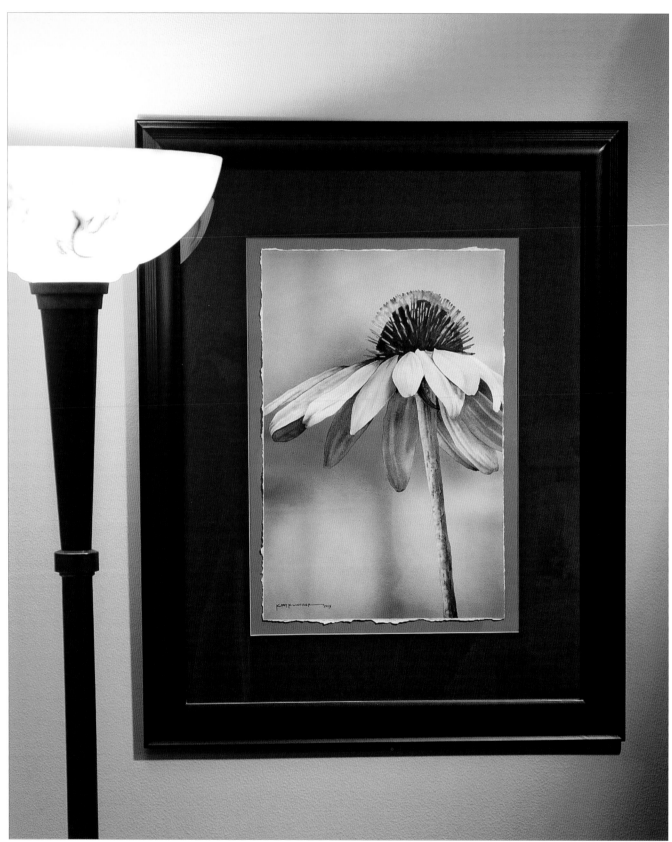

"Echinacea" 2003, 12½" x 19½"

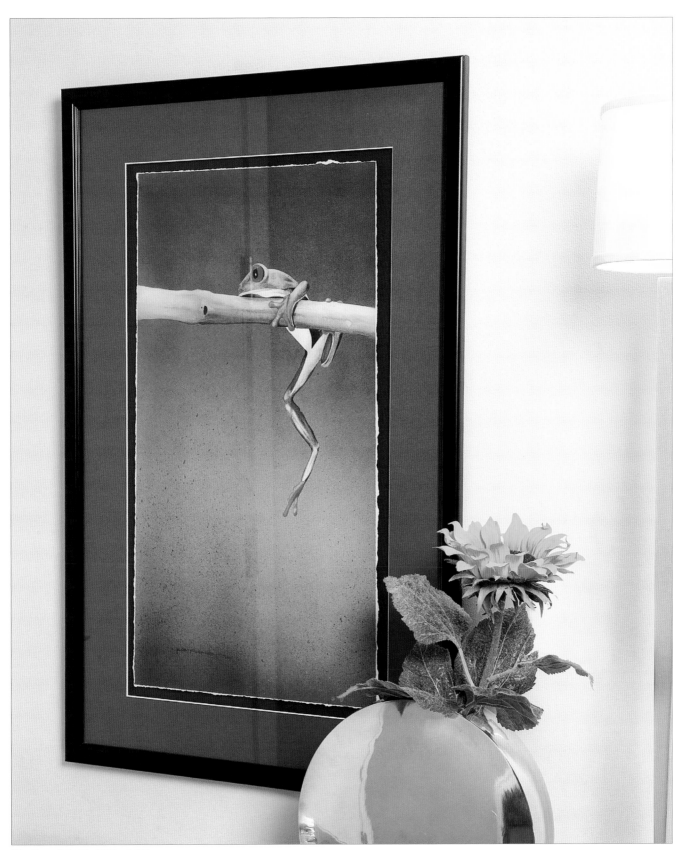

"La Rana" 2004, 12¼" x 24¼"

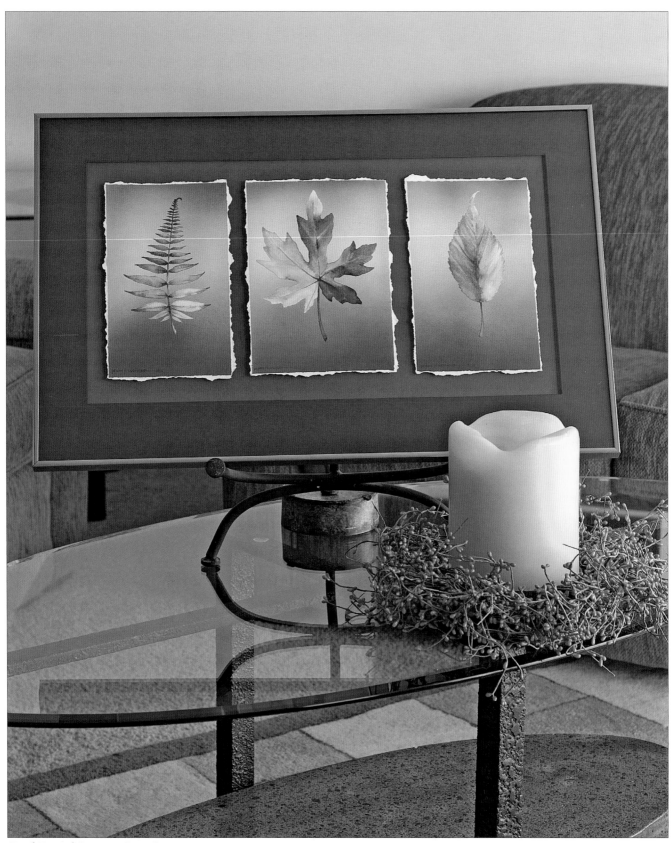

"Leaf Triptych" 2002, 19" x 10"

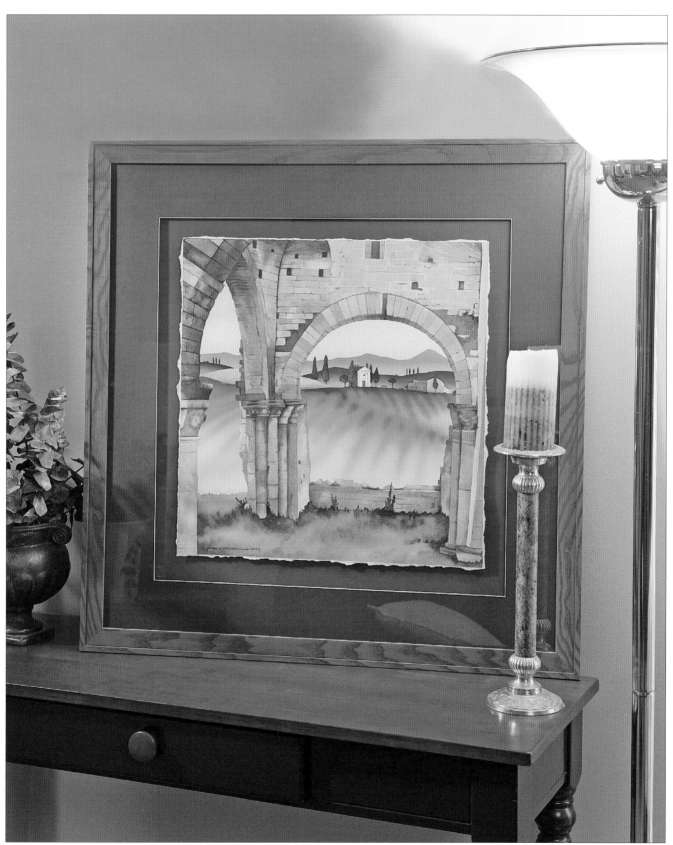

"Tuscan Arches" 2003, 20" x 20"

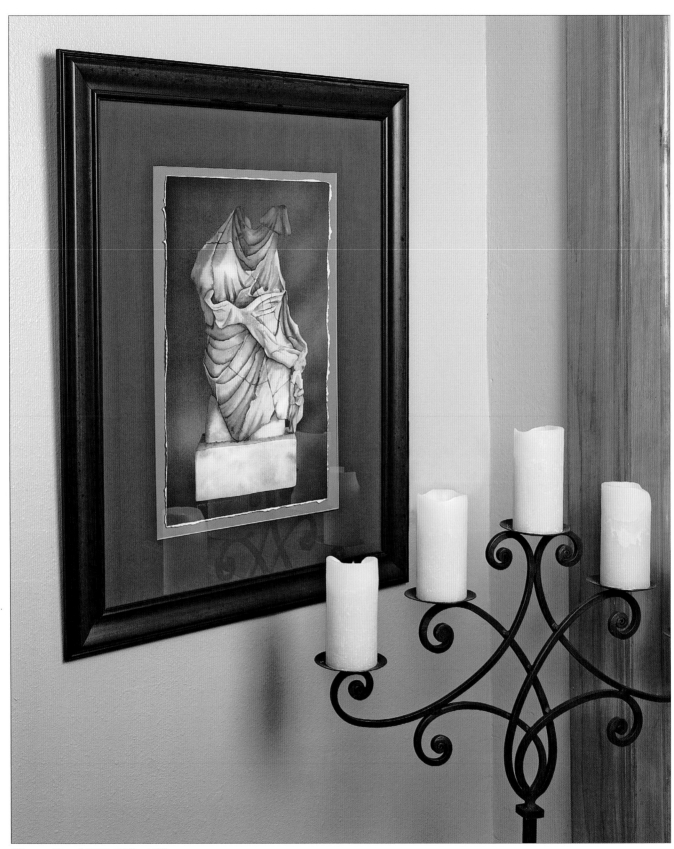

"Tuscan Torso" 2003, 10½" x 18½"

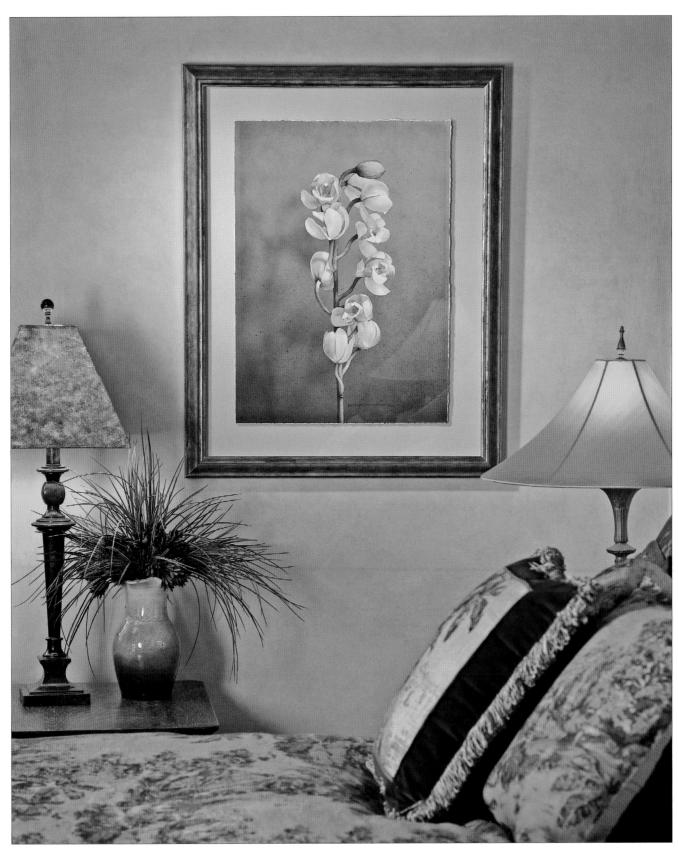

"Cymbidium" 2004, 19½" x 27"

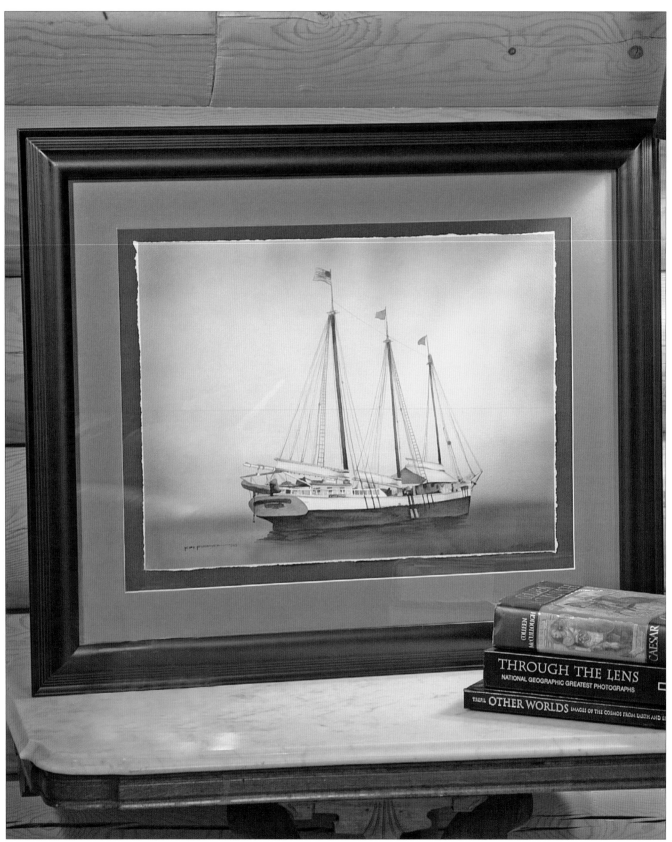

"Victory Chimes" 2003, 20¼" x 15"

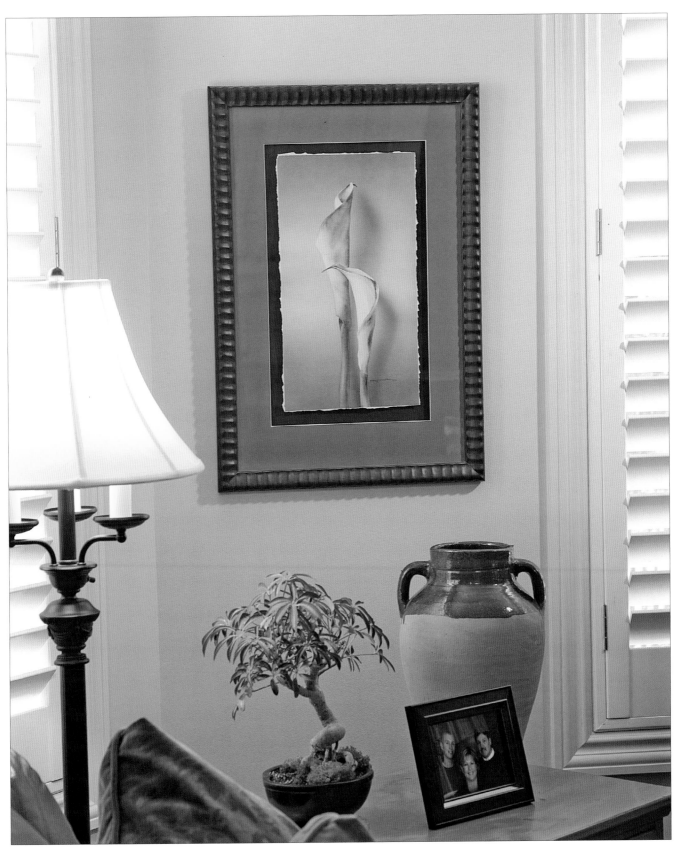

"Twin Callas" 2003, 10″ x 18½″

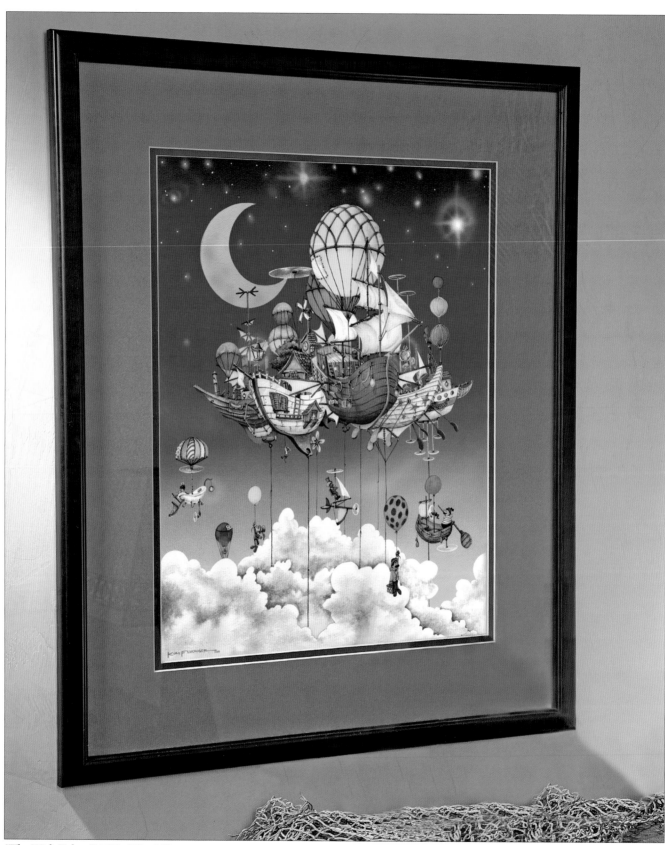

"The Wish Fishers" 2002, 18" x 24"

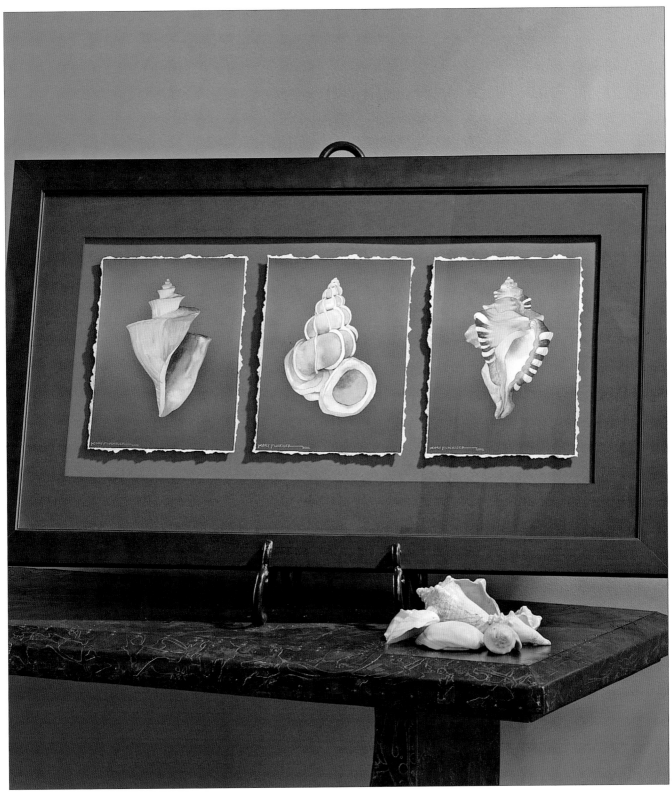

"Three Shells", 25½" x 10"

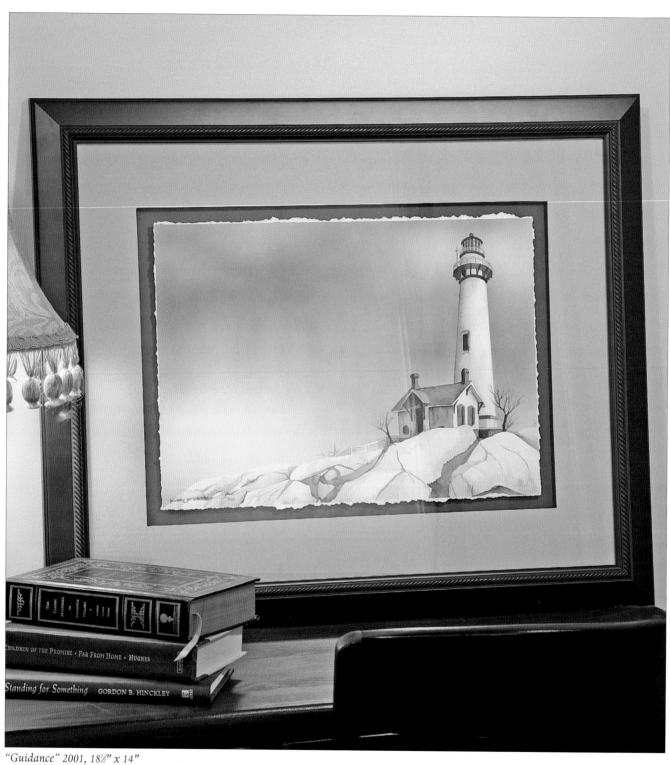

"Guidance" 2001, 18½" x 14"

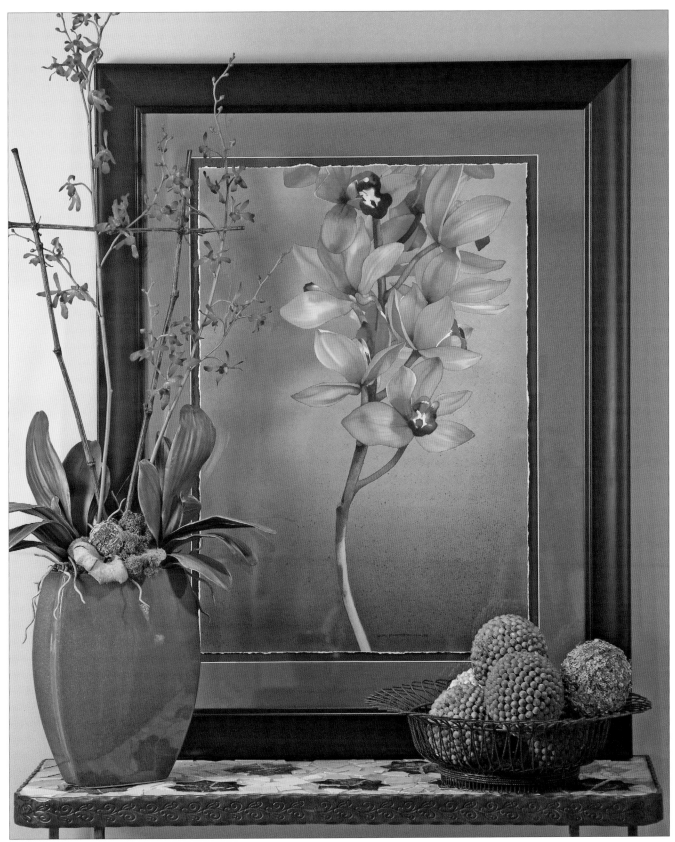

"Cymbidium Equinox" 2004, 19" x 27"

121

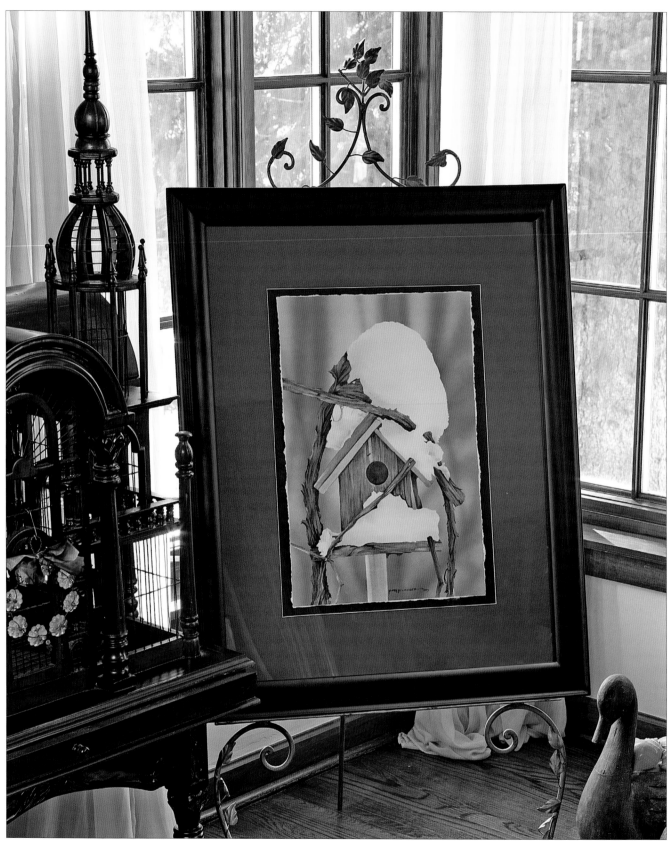

"Winter Quarters" 2003, 12½" x 19"

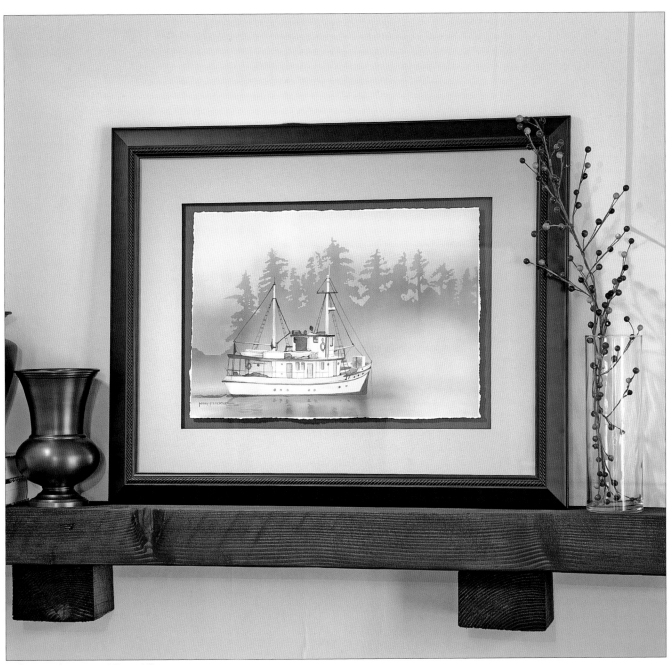

"The Sound" 2001, 19¼" x 12½"

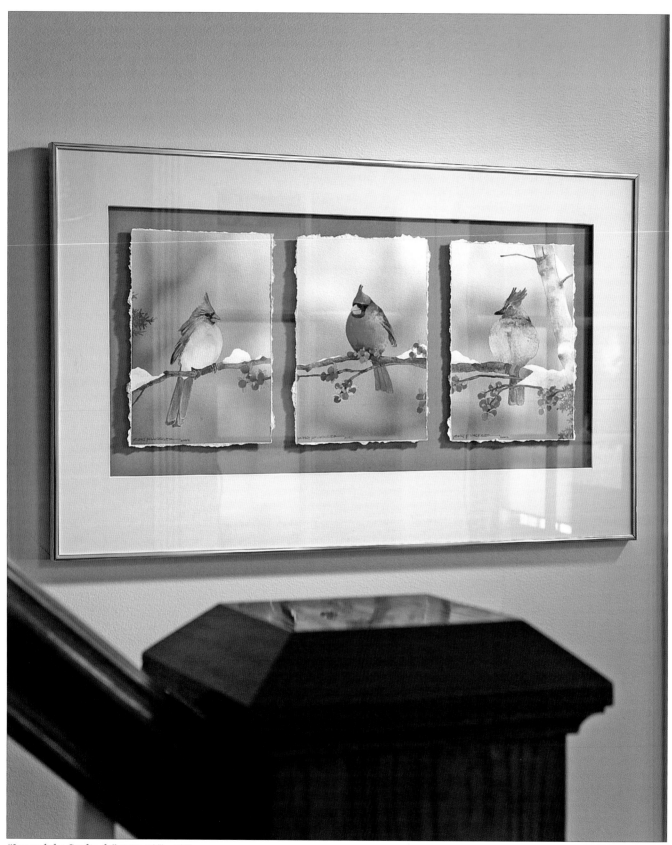

"Jay and the Cardinals" 2001, 9½" x 7½"

About the Author

Kory Fluckiger resides in Ogden, Utah, with his wife Heather McKinnon. Kory is primarily a self-taught artist and has been watercolor painting professionally since 2001. His work has been exhibited in several shows throughout Utah, including the Springville Art Museum, the Eccles Community Art Center, the Utah Arts Council traveling shows, and numerous other exhibitions, auctions, and charity events. *Utah Style & Design*, an interior decor magazine published in Salt Lake City, Utah, featured Kory in their Artisan Profile section of the Fall 2002 issue for his mural work, both commercial and private. Kory's paintings, limited-edition prints, and floral creations can be seen at Historic 25th Street's Olive & Dahlia in Ogden, Utah.

Kory's trademark watercolor style, with soft backgrounds and crisp, clear, isolated subjects, was self-developed in an attempt to stretch the medium beyond its presumed limitations. He believes that watercolors are generally underrated in their ability to express realism. He pushes himself with each painting to show otherwise. More of his original work as well as limited-edition prints can be seen on his Web site: www.koryfluckiger.com.

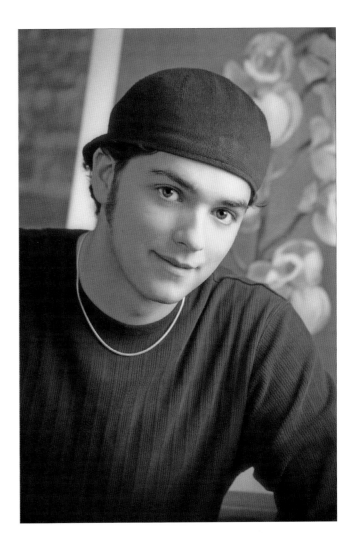

Resources

Fine Arts Gallery and Custom Framing
290 Historic 25th Street, Suite 101
Ogden, UT 84401
(801) 393-3771
www.FineArtson25th.com

Larson Juhl
6488 Gardenis Street
Arvada, CO 80004

Winsor & Newton
www.winsornewton.com

Acknowledgments

First, I would like to thank my wife Heather for being willing to share me with this project, which never could have been completed without her support and encouragement. I would also like to thank all of those people who enrich my life and inspire me on a daily basis—my friends and ever-supportive family, who come to every one of my shows, however small. Thank-you all!

I owe much to Dave Reese, my framer, a true artist in his craft, who designed and framed all of the projects in this book, and many of the gallery pieces. Thank-you for what you have given my work!

I would like to thank Larson Juhl for the frame supplies donated, and Winsor Newton for providing the watercolor supplies.

Thank-you, M. Emerson Robison, for shooting the bridal photograph used in the scrapbook project.

I would also like to extend my gratitude to the following people for allowing us to photograph parts of this book in their homes, and for allowing us to photograph the pieces of my artwork owned by them:

George and Barbara Dennis
Matt and Brooke Dennis
Evelyn Draper
London Draper
Kent and Stacy Frampton
Suzanne Lindquist
Jo Packham
Sue Schneider
Becky and Harry Senekjian
Casey and Anagay Shorten
Bonnie Smith
Barbara Ward
Linda Weiskopf

Editor: Ana Maria Ventura
Copy Editor: Marilyn Goff
Book Designer: Dan Emerson, Pinnacle Marketing
Photographers: Zac Williams, Chapelle Ltd., and Ryne Hazen, Hazen Photography
Photostylist: Kim Monkres

Metric Equivalency Charts

mm-millimeters   cm-centimeters
inches to millimeters and centimeters

inches	mm	cm	inches	cm	inches	cm
⅛	3	0.3	9	22.9	30	76.2
¼	6	0.6	10	25.4	31	78.7
½	13	1.3	12	30.5	33	83.8
⅝	16	1.6	13	33.0	34	86.4
¾	19	1.9	14	35.6	35	88.9
⅞	22	2.2	15	38.1	36	91.4
1	25	2.5	16	40.6	37	94.0
1¼	32	3.2	17	43.2	38	96.5
1½	38	3.8	18	45.7	39	99.1
1¾	44	4.4	19	48.3	40	101.6
2	51	5.1	20	50.8	41	104.1
2½	64	6.4	21	53.3	42	106.7
3	76	7.6	22	55.9	43	109.2
3½	89	8.9	23	58.4	44	111.8
4	102	10.2	24	61.0	45	114.3
4½	114	11.4	25	63.5	46	116.8
5	127	12.7	26	66.0	47	119.4
6	152	15.2	27	68.6	48	121.9
7	178	17.8	28	71.1	49	124.5
8	203	20.3	29	73.7	50	127.0

yards to meters

yards	meters	yards	meters	yards	meters	yards	meters	yards	meters
⅛	0.11	2⅛	1.94	4⅛	3.77	6⅛	5.60	8⅛	7.43
¼	0.23	2¼	2.06	4¼	3.89	6¼	5.72	8¼	7.54
⅜	0.34	2⅜	2.17	4⅜	4.00	6⅜	5.83	8⅜	7.66
½	0.46	2½	2.29	4½	4.11	6½	5.94	8½	7.77
⅝	0.57	2⅝	2.40	4⅝	4.23	6⅝	6.06	8⅝	7.89
¾	0.69	2¾	2.51	4¾	4.34	6¾	6.17	8¾	8.00
⅞	0.80	2⅞	2.63	4⅞	4.46	6⅞	6.29	8⅞	8.12
1	0.91	3	2.74	5	4.57	7	6.40	9	8.23
1⅛	1.03	3⅛	2.86	5⅛	4.69	7⅛	6.52	9⅛	8.34
1¼	1.14	3¼	2.97	5¼	4.80	7¼	6.63	9¼	8.46
1⅜	1.26	3⅜	3.09	5⅜	4.91	7⅜	6.74	9⅜	8.57
1½	1.37	3½	3.20	5½	5.03	7½	6.86	9½	8.69
1⅝	1.49	3⅝	3.31	5⅝	5.14	7⅝	6.97	9⅝	8.80
1¾	1.60	3¾	3.43	5¾	5.26	7¾	7.09	9¾	8.92
1⅞	1.71	3⅞	3.54	5⅞	5.37	7⅞	7.20	9⅞	9.03
2	1.83	4	3.66	6	5.49	8	7.32	10	9.14

Index